Local Government Website Management Methodology

AMMAR IBRAHIM SHIHAB

Dedication

To the great Messenger Mohammed may Allah grant peace and honor on him and his descendants.

Every challenging work needs self efforts as well as guidance of elders especially those who were very close to our heart.

My humble effort I dedicate to my sweet and loving.

Father & Mother,

Whose affection, love, encouragement and prayers of day and night make me able to get such success and honor,

Along with all hard working and respected

Supervisor

Acknowledgment

First of all, I thank my wife, Wafaa, for listening and supporting in the last couple of years. I deeply thank my supervisor, Prof. drhab.KesraNermend whose help, advice and supervision was invaluable.AlsoI deeply thank to Prof. drhab.DariuszZarzecki, expert in strategy in investment at the faculty of management and Dr. Jarosław Jankowski, whose help, advice and for some advice was invaluable. I also thank Dr. Barbara Wąsikow-skaand Dr.TomaszKomorowski whose help and cooperate in experiment, and Dr. An-naBorawska, who's commented and help to translate some text from Polish to English and versa during building new website. Finally, I would like to thank to Dr. Mateusz Piwowarski, whose help a give advice in my thesis.

Abbreviations

WCM	Web content management
CMS	Content management system
MCMS	Microsoft content management server
IS	Information system
IST	Information system technology
UFD	Usability, Friendliness, Design
ICT	information and communications technology
IA	Information architecture
DMS	data management system
SWOT	Strengths, Weaknesses, Opportunities, and Threats
EGOVSAT	Electronic Government Satisfaction Model
CSS	Cascading Style Sheets
DNS	Domain Name System
Q	Question
AVT	Average time
Char	Character
Bt	Binary Time
Bl	Binary links
Bq	Binary quality
LAU	Generally, a local administrative unit
NUTS	Nomenclature of Territorial Units for Statistics
FDI	Foreign direct investment
ICT	information communication technologies
NIE	New institutional economics
NAO	National Audit Office
CMPs	Community municipal portals in society
ICTs	information and communication technologies in society
ASPA	American Society for Public Administration
UNDPEPA	United Nations Division for Public Economics and Public Administration
G2G	Government to Government
G2B	Government to Business
G2C	Government to Citizen

G2E	Government to Employee
SOAP	Service object access protocol
WSDL	web service definition language
XML	Extensible Markup Language
UDDI	Universal description discovery and integration
UML	Unified modeling language
HCI	Human computer interaction
ID	Identification
U_k	Main Factors
S_i	Sub-Factors
VMCM	Vector measure construction method
σ_i	standard deviation of the i - th variable,
V_{x_i}	coefficient of significance
$\overline{x}_i$	mean value of the i - th variable,
x'_{i_w}	is the value of the i -th normalized variable for the pattern
$x'_{i_{k_1}}$	is the value of the i -th normalized variable for the first quartile
$x'_{i_{k_{III}}}$	is the value of the i -th normalized variable for the third quartile
$x'_{i_{aw}}$	is the value of the i-th normalized variable for the anti-pattern
V.B.Net	Visual Basic.Net
URL	Uniform Resource Locator
QNo.	Question Number
Qans	Question Answer
Qlty	Quality
Qtime	Quantity time
QLink	Quantity of links
QClass	Recognition webpage
Nc	Number of Characters
no links	Number of links
UID	User Identification
LGU	Local Government Units

X_1	is average of maximal number of users selecting the same web-page answer in time threshold
X_2	is average of the number of users who fall within the links threshold
X_3	is average of value of the average quality of information in webpage answer
X_4	is average of the value of average time answer
k	index of the vectors of X_1, X_2, X_3, X_4
i	index of the questions 1..5
j	index of the cities 1..8
WAN	Wide area network
LAN	Local area network
CMS	content management system
WCM	Web content management
FAQ	*Frequently Asked Questions*
DB	Database
KB	Knowledge base
U	User
Q	Question
Av	Average
UX	User experience
FUF	Flexibility, user-satisfaction, few error
WAI	web accessibility initiative

CONTENTS

INTRODUCTION

More and more people, representatives of business use websites of Local Government Units (LGU) to obtain information or to conduct administrative business. These websites ought to provide various categories of information in a clear and comprehensible manner for different groups of consumers. Each of these groups is interested in a particular content (information, documents, applications) which should be easily and intuitively accessed. For example, city-dwellers would be interested in administrative matters, opportunities to receive advice on administrative procedures, legislative issues and opportunities to conduct such business with the use of Internet applications. Tourists and visitors would look for information about tourist attractions, current and planned events, city life and accommodation. Another important group are investors who would search for information about investment opportunities in a city investment area, bids and auctions etc.). These groups of customers will include foreigners who have the same information needs like Polish residents (except for a part of city-dwellers). In addition to problems regarding information itself (what and how it is to be provided), there will also be problems connected with language versions, incomplete information in different languages or correctness of translation. People or foreign companies which could not find relevant information on a LGU website are often no longer willing to establish contact or even visit the place e.g. for tourism or education. The problem of usability of LGU websites is crucial as it directly shapes the image of a city and may also indirectly influence its development (in the fields of tourism, education, business). Needless to say, if information cannot be found on the Internet it is treated as if it never existed. After a few unsuccessful attempts the user quits the website what leads to loss of opportunities.

Local Government Units are therefore obliged to improve their website so that they customize to current and changing needs, concerning information at first. **A question may arise whether there is any guidance or standards regarding the structure of LGU websites and the scope and form of providing relevant information?**

Both in Polish and foreign literature on subject matter **there is not enough research which would include comprehensive studies of usability and relevance of the content and structure of LGU websites**. In case of commercial websites (e.g. E-commerce, websites advertising education etc.), one can more often experience their professional design which includes users' opinions on their usability. In case of LGU websites, financial constraints and lack of know-how prevent the use of professional design. Similar activity profile of all Local Government Units, similar content made available on websites, the same groups of consumers are reasons for creating a standard or, at least, guidelines regarding the design of structure and content of LGU websites. Guidelines or more preferably development of a high quality referential model of LGU website providing high usability would enable users to access desired content with relatively low cost.

The analysis of websites of provincial capitals in Poland has confirmed their imperfection in the context of information architecture and usability. As a result of this research, a number of problems have been identified:

- There is a distinct difference in the presentation of information between the Polish and English versions, and the use of automatic web-based translators may lead to poor service for foreign users.

- Language versions of Websites do not take into account differences in cultural communication of their customers (standards, customs, and communication within a given society).

- Potential investors, both local and foreign, encounter difficulty in finding information about investment and business opportunities in the local market.

- The inconsistent structure and information architecture of many websites results in their low usability.

The author of this dissertation decided to fill the existing gap by proposing the referential model of the LGU website (pattern), which would provide guidance both on the effective design of new LGU websites and optimisation of the existing ones. Scope and structure of the analysed issues require searching for solutions towards identification of important information categories which should be included in LGU websites and definition of their basic structure. The structure of the referential model of LGU website has to meet requirements relating to its standardization, to allow duplication (adjustment) of proposed solution to many other real-world situations (Internet websites of different local government units).

The main goal of this thesisis to create a referential model of a local government website containing relevant information for local and foreign users. The studied area refers to the three important subjects: **investments, business**and**tourism**. These three issues are important to local governments, since they allowincreasing income by attracting investors, businessmen and tourists. **Additional aims** include as following:

- The analysis of current local government websites in terms of relevance of information.

- The design of (website tracking) software which would analyse the access paths to information and time required by the user to get information.

The fulfillment of the aims of this research, i.e. guidelines for design and management of LGU websites, will provide methodological guidelines which may be used to design new LGU websites as well as improve existing ones. Creation of such methodological guidelines may lead to a standardization of structure and content of LGU websites. The existence of such a "model" would definitely facilitate design of user-friendly architecture and relevant content.

Partial aims of this research will be achieved through analysis of methodology of website evaluation, analysis of current LGU websites and creation of software (website tracking) which facilitates analytical processes of website usability.

The beneficiaries of these solutions will be both designers of such websites (information architecture, website usability) and LGU employees responsible for promotion, attracting of investors, tourism and businessmen (website content).

The established hypothesis states that use of the aggregate method and the examination of existing LGU websites enable development of a referential model of a website that includes information relevant to local and foreign users.

The research area of this dissertation has been aimed at issues related to design of usable Internet websites of LGU, including informative needs of their users' groups such as investors, businessmen, tourists.

This dissertation consists of five chapters. Chapter one includes discussion on the role of websites of local government units in the regional development and improvement of the quality of local government services. Chapter two is focused on content management systems, management of website content and issues relating to information architecture and websites usability. Chapter three describes methods and tools in the procedure of analysis and evaluation of local government websites. This chapter demonstrates also the web tracking system process including websites testing as well as the procedure for selection of LGU websites for further analysis. Chapter four, describes the researcher's method for testing usability of websites of local government units as well as the results of sub studies. Chapter five includes verification of usability of proposed referential model for LGU website.

The conclusions include summary of carried our surveys and results that validate the posed hypothesis.

Annex attached to the dissertation contains detailed research results and used empirical material.

Research procedure

To execute set objectives the research methodology presented in Fig. 1 was employed. This procedure involves several steps which result in the proposal of a model website dedicated for local government units.

Analysis of 20 LGU websites in terms of mechanisms and communication procedures

The next step of research will concern a check of response of officers responsible for the specific city information area to inquiries coming from foreign users. Inquiries will refer to investment opportunities and involve tourism (tourist attractions, accommodation facilities etc.). Therefore inquires of the specific content will be posted (via e-mail or contact forms from websites). The purpose of these activities will be practical verification of employed mechanisms and communication procedures via electronic channels applied on WWW under analysis. Availability of information desired by users on a website will also be verified.

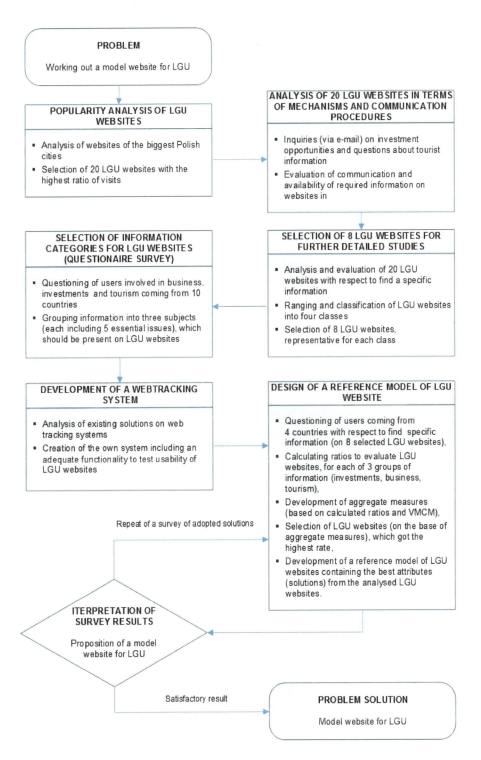

Fig.1. Research procedure applied to fulfill the work objectives.

Source: own elaboration

Selection of 8 LGU websites for further detailed studies

In the next step LGU websites selected in the previous stage will be subject to detailed evaluation in terms of possibility to find specific information. Thematic scope will refer to current investments being carried out by foreign investors, possibility to establish cooperation with local entrepreneurs, existing economic zones as well as tourism, education, transportation etc. Information contained on these 20 LGU websites will be scored from 0-9 (for each of adopted ratios) which will result in the observation matrix. Then using this matrix and applying VMCM method to develop an aggregate measure, these websites will be ranged and classified into 4 categories: very good, good, average, poor (according to the procedure proposed in the reference literature). 8 LGU websites, representative for the particular classes (2 websites of each class) will be selected as the effect of these activities.

Selection of information categories for LGU websites (questionnaire surveys)

The next step concerns determination and selection of particular groups of information which users (mainly foreigners) would expect to find on LGU websites. The selection of these groups of information will be made by respondents coming from different countries e.g. Malaysia, China, Dubai, Iraq, Saudi Arabia, Oman, USA, Sweden, Ukraine and Poland. There will be people involved in business, investments and tourism. They will be sent a questionnaire including a request to point at the most important information that is desired on LGU websites. Based on received responses information will be organized in 3 thematic groups (business, investments, tourism) of which each will contain 5 most important issues (according to respondents). Accessibility to this information will be tested using the web tracking system developed by the researcher.

Development of a web tracking system

The next stage of the work will include a design and implementation of a web tracking system built by the researcher. The aim of software development is to obtain a tool for measuring usability of LGU websites, including time needed to find information, tracking path to this information, number of links required to find information etc.

Design of a referential model of an LGU website

This step will involve testing users from different countries (using a new web tracking system created by the researcher) to find specific information on preselected 8 LGU websites. Among the others subject to examination will be time to receive an answer, number of clicks, number of people who reached the required information as well as flexibility of website, satisfaction of users and number of mistakes made while searching for information (scored 0-9).

The following ratios will be calculated on the base of users' surveys, separately for each of 3 thematic groups (investment, business, tourism):

X1 - the average time required to reach the relevant information;

X2 - the greatest number of users who will find the required information within the timeframe between the shortest and the average response time calculated for all responses.

X3 - the number of users who will find required information by number of clicks (in links to this information), falling within the interval between the least number of clicks and an average number calculated based on all clicks;

X4 - the average quality assessment of information provided by users evaluating content of a website.

On the basis of the summary of all ratios, with use of VMCM method 4 aggregate measures will be calculated:

- IM - aggregate measure of evaluation of a website for new investment using X_1 - X_4 ratios;

- BM - aggregate measure of evaluation of a website for already existing businesses using X_1 - X_4 ratios;

- TM - aggregate measure of evaluation of a website for people interested in tourism using X_1 - X_4 ratios;

- UFUF - aggregate measure of website usability evaluated by users under survey.

On the basis of aggregate measures, separately for 3 groups of information (investment, business, and tourism) and on the basis of UFUF usability measure (4 groups of measures) LGU websites which receive the highest score will be selected. The best solutions (attributes) will be implemented to the designed referential model of LGU website.

Interpretation of survey results

On the basis of the developed referential model of an LGU website the proposal of a model LGU website will be made. Then, the same survey will be carried out for this website in order to verify its solutions. The surveys will be similar to those performed in the previous step. The obtained results will be compared with results for the best solutions (out of 8 analysed LGU websites) from the previous step. The tests will aim at proving or not the aptness of the provided solution – the referential model of LGU website.

1. THE ROLE OF WEBSITES FOR LOCAL GOVERNMENT UNITS

1.1 Main tasks of local government units

Local government is a form of public management and administration, which in majority of contexts, issued as a term describing lower level of state administration (Regulski, 2003). Local government has law provided to it by some rule or directives of higher level of the government the institutions of local governments may differ between countries, and even if there is a similar system, the related terminology often varies.

The local governments may refer to state, town, borough, municipality, province, region, department, district, city, township, village, and local service district(Štaud, Ondřej, 2013; Bulkeley & Kern, 2006).

All local governments have legal subjectivity. The state government gives local government units authorisationto perform public duties, so-called tasks assigned.

The basic local government tasks include all public matters of local importance, particularly to meet the collective needs of the community living in the area. Tasks of localgovernmentunitsencompasses, amongothers(Friend & Jessop, 2013):

1) spatial management, real estate and environmental protection,
2) municipal roads, streets, bridges, squares and traffic organization,
3) water supply, sanitation, disposal and treatment, maintaining cleanliness and order and supply of electricity, heat and gas,
4) telecommunications,
5) local public transport,
6) health care and social assistance,
7) education, culture and tourism, public policy, family policy, etc.

Regional government is responsible for the regional development policy which consists of:1) Creating conditions for economic development, including labor market policy,2) The maintenance and development of social and technical infrastructure importantfor the whole province,3) Acquiring and combining public and private funds to carry out public tasks,4) Carrying out activities to raise the level of education of citizens,5) The rational use of natural resources and environmental development depending on the principles of sustainable development, etc.

Tasks related to professional activation are carried out in part by the local government system of social assistance including social welfare centres and district social assistance centres. These units may perform entrusted tasks e.g. through cooperation with entrepreneurs.

There are five areas of local government activities that affect the investment atmosphere in the area (Brzezinski, 2009). These are the following:

1) regulatory and legal,
2) information and promotion,
3) investment and organizational,
4) financial and redistribution,
5) coordination and conciliation.

Local government units may assist entrepreneurs, including foreign investors, using the instruments of state aid. Such assistance may be an additional precondition for investors when deciding on the location of an economic activity. Support offered to foreign investors also takes another form. Provision of information is important, but relatively the simplest and least time-consuming. Besides, local government supports foreign investors by developing infrastructure (Drożyński & Urbaniak, 2011).

Local government plays an important role in the economy of the country. According to the Constitution of the Republic of Poland local government carries out the essential part of public tasks(Demczuk & Pawłowska, 2006).

Local government duty is to increase revenue focusing on three important factors investment, business and tourism - in such forms like increasing public revenue for the city through incentives for foreign investors and development of tourist facilities (Fjeldstad& Heggstad, 2012). In addition, in the framework of agricultural and industrial projects revenue can be increased by raising the export standard. Local governments have responsibilities with regard to dynamic growth in local enterprises through decentralization processes that occur in EU, including also Poland. This refers to the responsibility of local authorities which are obliged to implement public projects on the local level(Skica et. al.,2013).The municipalities may introduce local restrictions that have not been legally applicable to other units.These restrictions and facilitation may refer to the following fields:

1) social infrastructure (i.e. schools, social care, health care),
2) technical infrastructure (i.e. roads, water supply, sewage system),
3) public order and security (i.e. fire protection, mass events security, civil security),
4) spatial and ecological order (i.e. air, water, forests, land protection and waste management).

The several of commune tasks have an open character and comprise all activities that are important for local communities. Taking into considerations that economic development at the micro level is significant for quality of life, it allows assuming that tasks which aim at support entrepreneurship may be financed from public funds. One of these elements is to "make conditions for economic developments, including labor market" (Foley et. al.,2015).

Tasks of local authority include also support to local entrepreneurship and creating conditions to attract investment capital(Skica et. al.,2013; Rafal & David, 2011).

The factors influencing entrepreneurship development and indirectly affect development of local government unitsarepresented in Table 1.1.

Table 1.1 Factors influencing entrepreneurship

Factors influencing entrepreneurship	Factors restraining entrepreneurship
− ease of setting up a new company − cheap and highly educated labour − easy access to knowledge − communication access − transparent tax regime − availability of low cost bank loans − access to new technologies − cheap energy carriers − supportive attitude of local authorities − stable political situation	− high loan rates − lack of stable government policy towards entrepreneurs − highlabour costs − instability of employment law regulations − corruption − instable fiscal policy − technical and economic infrastructure on the low level of development − long period of return on investment − lack of spatial development plan

Source: T. Skica A. BemK. Daszyńska-Żygadło. The role of local government in the process of entrepreneurship development, e-Finanse,University of Information Technology and Management, Financial Internet Quarterly , vol. 9/no 4, p. 1-24, 2013.

Local governments have far moreimpact on organizational and interactive factors. Thisis related to the widely defined efficiency of localauthority activities. Factors highly influencing local units include technical infrastructure, quality of service in local government offices, attitude of citizens and of local authorities towards investments. These factors are crucial for investors in the investment decision making process (Picot & Wernick, 2007).

The task of the local authorities is to provide better, customer-oriented and more efficient public services. Enabling citizens and businesses to transact electronically with government organizations and agencies is thekey part of this strategy (Ustawa PZP,2004).

Local governance is a broader concept and is defined as the formulation and execution of collective action at the local level(Gilbert & Richard, 2013).The goal of local government service is the facilitation of the transaction between the government, citizens, and businesses as presented in figure 1.1.The number of e-services in local government is available and their quality therefore can be considered a measurement for the development level of local government website(Krishnan et. al., 2012; Zheng & Lu, 2012).

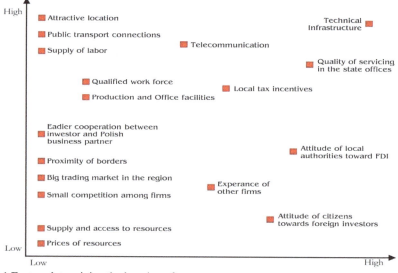

Fig. 1.1.Factors determining the location of a company.

Source: Dziemianowicz, W. Rola władz samorządowych w przyciąganiu kapitału zagranicznego. In: Z.Olasiński (Ed.), Bezpośrednie inwestycje zagraniczne w Polsce, PWE,1998.

Over the recent years digital local government (or local government website) is becoming a very active and makes fast progress in development by research area with lots of promises to revolution government and its interaction with customers, in addition interaction with businesses, citizens, and other reference. Local government website means electronic government (Gamper & Augsten, 2003; Yavuzet. al., 2014). Technological developments allows to conversions of all types of communications to a digital format. This includes documents, forms, letters, books, newspapers, professional journals, speech, telephone cells, television, movies, photographs, and music. The infrastructure in the www allows for storage, transmission, and provides ability to share these types of technical materials electronically. The bandwidth available for transmission and our ability to convert materials and make use of them is growing. Local electronic government(LEG) exploits these abilities and processes to enhance governmental effectiveness(Streib &Willougbby, 2002). Local government websites, are also referred to aslocal government websites, which can support the civil and political administrations through information and communication technologies(Elmagarmid & McIver, 2001)

The public face of a local government for the purpose of facilitating the services provided to both citizens and investors is its own website. Where advertisements of services, investment and tourist attractions are published and information to people is provided easily and quickly. It is also the public face presented to the world to invite and attract the foreign investment to the city(Hong, 2013).

The Internet is being used as the core delivery channel for enabling these improvements in service delivery. With its associated open standards and technologies, the Internet provides a major means of establishing electronic relationships between government organizations and their customers(Sebek, 2003). Local government website involves using information and communication technology to deliver public services through digital channels (Flak et. al., 2003).The role of local government website in economic development has been extensively studied. There are many of existing researches on the economic developments of activities in local governments(Morgan, 2009; Caulfield & Larsen, 2013).

Websites for local governments differ from those of companies, where the first are focused on supporting and providing services to citizens, investors and aim to increase the revenue of the city from the three important sources (investment, business, and tourism), while websites of companies focus on the profit as the primary goal. Therefore, local governments are trying to be specific in the construction and development faced by the world through the development of their websites in order to increase trust between citizens and local government(Henrikssonet al., 2007).

1.2 Specific of web-based services of local government units

Over the past decennium, the revolution in the provision of local government website services to citizens has been seen (Moon, 2002). While information communication technologies (ICT) make it possible to development and deploy local government website services, there are attracting attention differences in the reasons beyond varying levels of local government use in different countries. While developed countries, e.g., USA and many European countries, make progress in to infrastructures of ICT, local government website services usage by citizens is still limited(Baqir & Iyer, 2010).

Local government website provides extensively of government services by using Web portals (i.e., e-services). The number of e-services provided in the local government website portal is growing(Fang &Sheng, 2005). Although local government is generally the least innovative, all levels of government are interested in utilizing this approach to deliver services (Wang et. al., 2005).

Development of the Internet is the process of interaction within a group of cooperatinglocal governments. This process enables citizens to track and trace the status if the interface and access to the site and evaluate the application the modification onsite (Hoogwout & Marcel, 2003).

An accessible website is the one which makes no obstacles for users to access its contents. It provides full-value information to anyone independently from their abilities, health conditions or technical equipment(Plessers, 2005; Detlor et. al., 2013).

Globalization process influencing of the form and functions of the cities in different ways and creates a competitive environment between them in order to integrating them into the global networks (Castells, 2008). The trends in globalization and localization change services and the way they are delivered within the structure of public administration, thereby bringing up the requirements for the reconstructions of public administrations(Bekir et. al., 2008).

In Poland, basic Internet access to public administration was introduced in 2001 through the Public Information Bulletin (*BiuletynInformacjiPublicznej*). The bulletin consists of a Unified system of Internet websites, established and maintained for providing public information (Pawel & Banas, 2010). During this process, local government structures are emphasized despite the seemingly more logical concept that the "global leads the local" more easily in this emphasis, it is not an obstacle to the development of the local governments website. With this purpose, it can be seen that international organizations and developed countries give special priority to the concepts of subsidiarity, decentralized construction, local democracy, and participation of the non-governmental organizations in the local policy-making process, local autonomy, and governance (Shatkin, 2000; Garnik, 2006; Mimicopouloset. al. 2007).

Today, in addition to strengthening local governments by increasing the facilities of the local non-governmental organizations, supporting the local media, overcoming the entrepreneurs have some of obstacles experienced, increasing the effective participation of the local community in the decision-making process, encouragement local government unions can be increasing local governments' abilities to cooperate with the international organizations and unions, and transferring authorities from the provincial units to the local governments can be considered within the trend of localization (Bekir et. al. 2008).

The defined of local government website as the use of information and communication technology (ICT) as a means to improve quality, efficiency, and transparency of service delivery in the public administration. Since its inception systems were aware of the importance of the human factor at the stage of the system and its operation. Therefore Appears a system definition which says it is made up of hardware, software and human ware. The measures of development, popularization and increasing the systems noted a decisive influence on the success of an ICT system is firstly to adapt its functionality to meet the needs of users and secondly friendship servicing the way that it provides the user (usefulness - Important information concerning human interaction with computer system (Filutowicz & Przybyszewski, 2014).

Currently, there is no one common definition for local government website. The UN Division for Public Economics and Public Administrations defines local governments websites as "utilizing the Internet and the www for providing government services and information to citizens(Abanumy, 2006). Similarly the United Kingdom National Audit Office (NAO) defines it as" electronic or local government website means providing public access via the Internet to information about all the services offered by central government departments and their agencies; and enabling the public to conduct and conclude transactions for all those services (Argetts & Patrick, 2002). Some of local governments are working with community agencies in their jurisdictions to create a single-point of online access and providing citizens with a place in one-stop access to a through electronic suite of municipal government and society based on information and services (Brian et. al., 2013). The community municipal portals (CMPs) are different from local government websites, the portal content contributions from community agencies in that local government's jurisdiction.

As the role and utility of local government websites becomes increasingly important, local governments need to launch successful websites that provide citizens with quality of information and services preferred. The better understanding the role quality of information in CMP can be adoption and use holds great potential in helping local governments realize this goal(Brian et. al., 2013; Keet. al., 2004).

Many countries often considered to combine local governments to lower service-delivery costs, increase accountability, improve service quality, and improve market equity, or enhance contribution in government system.Concept of local government is to make them more independent, provide more autonomy. That is, can offer them more power to act within, and formalize their institutional framework by upholding all the benefits of local government through elected representatives (Rahman, 2010). Thus, making a range of critical information publicly available, for example, on a city website, improves the possibility of good governance and can lead to better quality of life. Better information provides better means to control public accountability, and cities can do a lot using web technology to improve the access to information (Léautier, 2006).

The information technology in local governments are witnessing rapid and widespread in the communities, the economy and governments. They differ in nature, habits, culture, practice, states, and habitations between societies, regions and nations (Rahman, 2010). Local government units have to investing the interactive possibilities of the Internet, especially to support its role in the rise of democratic participation.

Local governments are in a more advantageous position than other public authorities, at least in fulfilling two important functions. Firstly, the local government units transform to be a special means to manage the democratic but politicized conflicts that flat the way for the realization of participation in the local level. Secondly, they function as public institutions with a role in the local service production-distribution and in the solution of problems related to local interests(Bekir et. al.,2008).

Although there is extensive attention in local government website. The local government website may not have a consistent. The revolutions in business, is often related with governments and through IT. In specially website technology which can be enhanced internal and external process in qualifications, abilities and service providing to the citizens(Laswadet. al., 2005).

The web-based Government-to-Citizen relationship demands certain drivers; amongst these is the availability of Internet services, which are considered as the primary drivers for local governments' website implementation. Therefore many public organizations in countries around the world are working to embrace the WWW for delivering information and services to citizens. This is because the Internet is rapidly increasing in usage. It is considered as one of the most efficacious means of helping in disseminating government information electronically. It has also changed the manner of worldwide communication (Dunleavy et. al., 1999). Local government websites generally focusing on improving the information and services provided to the citizens, business and governments. The expectation, associated with local government website implementation, is that government will improve its efficiency and enhance the delivery of information and services to a citizen. The major benefit of having an online presence through the Internet to LGU website users is to enable public organizations to provide a fast and easy way to use the system of delivering information and services on a 24hr per day basis. Local government website applications provide LGU website users, with the flexibility to seek the information they need or to conduct transactions, e.g. filling in online forms outside standard government office hours. Also, LGU would help citizens to reduce travel and waiting time to either ask for information, or conduct a transaction.

Comprehensive understanding of a role of LGUs websites includes all aspects of management and administration (respecting public opinion, decision-making, creation and provision of public services). These are processes existing in these units and they can be supported by using of information and communication technologies. The lowest level in hierarchy with regard to these processes refers to communication, administrative contacts between citizens and local government. There it is decided to what extent the authority acts as a service-provider and not just a governmental body(Karkin, 2014).

The main purpose to create a website by a local government unit is to improve administration and communication with citizens. The main effect of local government website is simply to implement better policy, more understandable to citizens, provision of higher quality services, but also involving citizens in development of local communities (Wilson & Game, 2011).

The factors that guarantee success of a design of a LGU website, so called virtual town hall, can be sub-divided into five categories:

1) specifics of requirements to design the virtual town hall - on one hand (vision, strategy, goals) and on the other hand the efficient project management,
2) content of information, provided services, functions which will be available on a virtual town hall website and their users functionality,
3) personnel, technical infrastructure, financing of a virtual town hall,
4) exchange of experience during execution of similar projects, partnership for projects,
5) factor of legality.

Figure 1.2.Illustrates factors influencing the success of innovative solutions in e-administration.

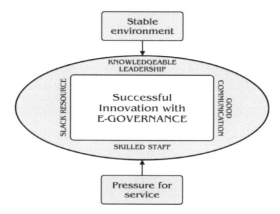

Fig.1.2. Factors to introduce e-administration

Source: Gregory D. Streib, Katherine G. Willougbby, Local government becoming local government website, Georgia state University, USA, 2001, hand book, chapter 13, P201.

The success of a local government unit's webpage can be measured to the extent in which the set objectives have been achieved. Development of a user -friendly LGU website is a single activity. Over the operation time of such a website activities aiming at updating to current users' needs should be carried out on a permanent basis. Long-term involvement both with regard to technical maintenance and development and editorial supervision over the content published on webpages is thus required (Staebner& Marchand, 2012).

The ASPA and UNDPEPA,The American Society for Public Administration and United Nations Division for Public Economics and Public Administration define local e-government as "Utilization the internal and the Web to provide LGUs website information and service to the citizens" (UNDPEPA, 2002). Depending on the UN, there are five main steps to build a LGUs website. Weakness in the organization of the site to be taken into consideration is **zero stage**(Gichoya, 2005; Carterb & Bélanger, 2005).

1) Initial web presence, which contains static information as a type of online guide. The aim is to provide an online mechanism of communicating key to give information about government to the citizens. The website may poorly of information about services or may be not organized pattern what people focused on.

2) Essential role of the information associated with the service can be more powerful in the website presence, as well as the means of communication that supported sites as a means of communication between the components of society. However, not everything is available to the user, offering limited contact with the amount of information about services provided by the government, which would be inadequate and what to look forward to the citizen of the local government website.

3) Web effectiveness, initialized to proceed in domain of local government website related with the citizens. Basically, the information is depicted by intuitive groupings that cross agency lines. For example, the website might use a portal as the single point of entry into various departments and service areas. The portal can offer major grouping like business, seniors, new resident, children, or other standard groups. Then, the end user would select the grouping that applies and be launched into a new section of the portal where the most common services requested for the group are located. The services could not be listed by departmental areas, but in fact by functional areas. Stage Three sites have to down-

loadable forms with online submissions, email contact for various governmental agents, and links to other local government websites (Reddick, 2004).

4) Public website can offer the ability to conduct secure online commercial transactions. This stage is also organized by user needs and contains dynamic information. The local government website may offer various commercial transactions, including paying for services, paying taxes, and paying bills. Transactions in web turnout included online submission of forms, many downloads, e-mail contact, and several links to other governments. The digital signatures also can be within contents of this step.

5) Although this stage represents an ideal, there is no real example of its application. Stage five involves a cross-agency, intergovernmental approach that only displays one front, regardless of service area. For example, local governments website would provide local, state, and federal government services via the state portal without the end user recognizing what level of government offering the services. Stage five a site would offer vertical and horizontal integration and would require true organizational transformation with respect to administrative boundaries (Schelin, 2007; Kim & Bretschneider, 2004).

Over the last 10 years LGU websites were subject to significant modifications and evolution. In common understanding local government websites provide such information and communication technologies that ensure faster, cheaper, easier, and more efficient access to information and various services than through traditional means of communication. Such methods are desired both by citizens, enterprises and organizations of different type e.g. non-profit but also other local or state government entities(Baqir & Iyer, 2010). Applied Information and Communication Technologies (ICT) include not only technical aspects of local government units but also refer to solutions used by local networks. These and other ICT areas are linked to the level and dynamics of a local social and economic development(Owsiski & Ponichtera, 2010).

Generally, most of local government websites follow design guidelines of commercial websites, focused on commercial activity. Copying of solutions is used in spite of the fact that these two types of websites have different characteristics and consumers. Guidelines to design e-administration websites should be developed in a slightly different way; they should be in accordance with the scope of conducted activity. The designers should develop a conceptual model that satisfies users' needs. The government website should primarily consider the needs of users and be coherent to the users' mental model(Kim et. al., 2007).

1.3   Thematic Scope of Local Government Units Websites

The concept of web-based information content assessment framework of local government websites basically consists of three components: information content, design and organisation (Abanumy, 2006). The information content component focuses on information issues of what should be included on LGU websites and refers to quality of such information. The design component involves issues related to web-based information content in the context of website usability and website accessibility. The third component refers to factors that affect web-based information content creation on local government websites inside public organizations. Fig 1.3 shows the general overview of the web-based information content assessment framework.

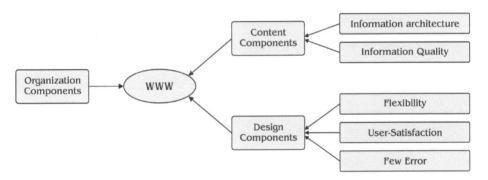

Fig. 1.3.Overview of the conceptual web-based information content assessment framework.

Source:Abanumy A.,Developing a framework for assessing quality of local government websites of Saudi ministries(Doctoral dissertation, University of East Anglia), 2006.

LGU websites are published in the most developed form (as presented in Fig. 1.4), include all management and administration aspects (creation of public policy, making decisions, development and service provision). They are provided as a long-term process with support of advanced information and communication technologies.

Webpages of LGU are used to provide basic information concerning e.g.: budgetary and registration issues, terms of sessions, meetings etc. but also sharing services, expression of opinions, which are further used in a process of taking decision(Institute for local government, 2012).

This particularly includes seamless transactions between the administration and its customers and a well-developed participation of citizens in the local community policy formation and decision-making processes via the Internet and new media(Drüke, 2004).

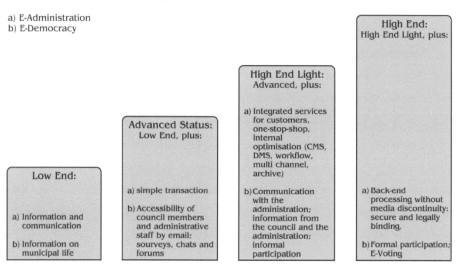

Fig.1.4. Four levels of local government website support by ICT technology.

Source: Helmut Drüke, Local Electronic Government, A comparative study,First published 2005 by Routledge, London and New York, pp1-283,p237.

Local government website in its most developed form, i.e. "High end local government website" (see Figure 1.4), means that all aspects of government and administration (public policy formation, decision-making, development and provision of services, participation) are supported by information and communication technology to a large extent (Rogerson, 2011). This particularly includes seamless transactions between the administration and its customers and a well-developed participation of citizens in the local community policy formation and decision-making processes via the Internet and new media(Helmut, 2005). Measured by these standards, local government website throughout the developed world is now on the threshold of transactions after the first stages of development in which the focus was on the creation of municipal information systems such as administrative guidance, forms, municipal portals and facilities for communication (email, chats, etc.).Simple transactions such as resident registration after birth or in the case of address change, as well as company registration, are well spread. Developed transactions exist in only a few cases(Helmut, 2005).

Advanced individualized transactions such as payment of taxes and charges and e-procurement are relatively far developed in those countries in which the statutory and technical obstacles in relation to transaction security, legally binding transactions and authenticity are relatively low(Chen & Thurmaier, 2008).

Therefore, once available online for downloading or viewing, public servants no longer have to individually provide specific information included in the program. In this way public access to information is secured and thus the legal obligation fulfilled. The great advantages of introducing ICT to reduce the load on bureaucracy may clearly contribute to transform traditional Weberian (Weberian model is related to administrations in an organization. It's main features which can be found in large organization, strict adherence to laws and regulations may increase the bureaucracy, government officials are appointed on merit basis)(Fountain, 2004). The latter relies on information technologies, electronic communication, digital documents in a flexible form, maintained and transmitted electronically, and rapid, real-time processing. Unfortunately, this win situation for both the public and the administration in many municipalities remains still merely an ideal.

Networked developments in mathematics and computing may change the flow of work, reducing and transforming traditional "Weberian" bureaucracy into virtual one has been characterized (Pawlowska et. al., 2002; Boley et. al., 2014):

- information structured by information technology rather than people,
- electronic and informal communication,
- maintain electronic files and transmitted in flexible and save it in form electronically,
- cross-functional and empowered employees,
- roles embedded in applications and information systems,
- rapid or real-time processing,
- constant monitoring and updating of feedback.

Recognizing rules of governance implies informing citizens and/or clients on hearing response and public affairs to them. It means performing deliberate information policy either through traditional media or new ones, i.e. Internet. It also means delivering public services in a new, more comprehensive, up to date way. Study recognize governance and Internet as the primary factors transforming virtual bureaucracy into local government website(Meurs et. al.,2013). Networked databases made public servant in the institution to be able to offer a wide range of information as well as to modify and retrieve citizens documents, often in real time (Margetts& Dunleavy, 2002).

Website content for local agencies to consider:1- Decision-Making Information, 2- Financial and Human Resource Information, 3- Elected Official Information.

Early experiences in application of local government website has established an idea that government should be an economic-driven organization, and set three bases for local government website:1 - Introduction of outcome-based approaches,2 - Utilization of market mechanisms and3 - Fulfillment of customer-centric environment(Lowe, 2003; Wagner et. al., 2006; Kelton & Pennington, 2012).

Conventional government organizations often prioritize securing budgets. However ultimate results are the most important aspect Therefore, transformation to outcome-based approaches with necessary evaluation using clear benchmarks was introduced (Prabhu, 2013). The next concept is utilization of market mechanisms. Businesses in government can be classified into two groups: businesses essentially belong to government, and businesses that are suitable for the private sector. This is an idea that overall business efficiency in government can be improved by demarcating public and private business fields. The third concept is fulfillment of customer-centric environment this idea involves treating citizens as customers of public services and pursuing customer satisfaction. The concepts and objectives of local government website are changing as time goes on(Prasad & Shivarajan, 2015). The Objectives of LGU includes:

- better manage public service to increase quality of life,
- government can dealing with modernized business process and each electronically other,
- a census through LGUs website can be important to the future,
- the citizen can access to LGUs website services at times and taking account special needs and social,
- improving operational qualifications in the government,
- improve transparency in government through information disclosure.

Implementation of websites in local government units can be classified into four phases, namely (Kaaya, 2001):

- website creation,
- provision of two side way interaction,
- adding opportunity to make online transactions,
- creation of extensive websites of local authorities.

In the first phase, local government websites are used to provide information and simple services to citizens only. The second phase focuses on building a platform to increase interaction between citizens and government. Creation of web tools to facilitate various service transactions is the third phase. The fourth phase is an integration of government systems with systems used in local government units. Usability factor in local government websites is particularly important in phases one and two of the implementation of LGU's website. Web usability means that it is simple and user-friendly (Cappel & Huang, 2007).

Internet information improves the relevance of searches from the consumer's perspective. This helps to eliminate much of the complexity and challenges of trying to predict or guess how a citizen may view or want to search for specific information or services. If users are allowed to tag contents, then some form of authentication is necessary to assure "correctness", and this can require significant time and effort. Different maturity models for local government website have been developed. Generally speaking, these models tell us that "the more LGUs website the better", but these models predict a linear, stepwise, and progressive development of LGUs website without taking into account the fact that more local government website also requires more experience. In fact, it implies moving from one stage to another, which requires changes, and that includes more and different challenges for organizations to deal with (Gomes & Sousa, 2012).

Well-developed structure and functionality of local government website enables public sector organizations to achieve relevant benefits through delivery of efficient services at the local or state level. Use of Information and Communication Technology (ICT) in construction of local government units websites allow increasing of quality and availability of services offered by LGU. For this purpose more and more mobile devices, i.e. smartphones are being used in this respect(Zambrano, 2009; Goldkuhl & Persson, 2006).

Web-based services provide a new layer of abstraction over existing software systems, capable of make bridging to any operating system, programming language or any hardware platform. Even though the Web is mainly for human users, Web services provide a framework for program to program communication. Web-based services are basically adapters between distributed applications, which allow to map messages into a canonical format and to send them across the Internet. Through the widespread adoption of this technology applications at various Internet locations can be directly interconnected as if they were part of a single, large information system(Gamper & Augsten, 2003; Ebrahim et. al., 2003).

In contrast to traditional IT systems, which can be characterized as tightly coupled systems, Web services implement a loosely coupled approach (Kleijnen & Raju, 2003). A Web services framework is consisting of three basic services: communication, service description and service discovery.

The basic functionality can be implemented protocols. There are three basic standards within the Web services framework for these protocols "object access protocolSOAP", "web service definition language WSDL" and "Universal description discovery and integration UDDI", all based on the common XML Meta language. Figure 1.5 shows a graphical overview over the interaction concept of these protocols, in the notation of an UML component diagram (Elsas, 2003).

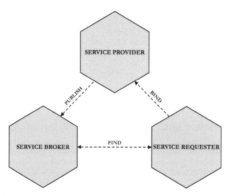

Fig. 1.5.Service Orientation.

Source: Alexander Elsas "Integration of Local government website and E-Commerce with Web Services", Institute for Information Systems, Goethe-University Frankfurt, EGOV 2003, LNCS 2739, Springer-Verlag, Berlin Heidelberg, Germany,2003, pp. 373–376.

eService is a core component in the LGUwebsite domain because it bridges the gap between the government administrators and citizens. Figure 1.6 shows "eService" as one of the main actors in LGU website domain; where arrows indicate "influence", circles indicate "domains of control" and intersection of circles indicates "transactions zones" (Bhuiyan, 2011).

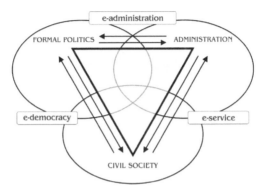

Fig. 1.6.eService as a component in LGU website domain.

Source: Bhuiyan, M.S.H "Public Sector eService Development in Bangladesh: Status, Prospects and Challenges" Electronic Journal of e-Government Volume 9 Issue 1 2011, (pp15 - 29), available online at www.ejeg.com

The size and complexity of the public administration, the inhomogeneous infra-structure, the different competences at the political level and the need for different services in different places require a powerful mechanism to interconnect different authorities at the application level. Web services have the potential to solve the information integration problem of LGUs website(Gamper & Augsten, 2003; Kwak et. al., 2003).

2. USABILITY OF WEBSITE CONTENT

2.1 Basic concepts and definitions on systems of content management

Many organizations have created a Web site and most have established some infrastructural support for their Web site, such as a Web manager or a Web services department. There has been an explosion of content on Web sites as the potential of the Web for internal and external communication is recognized. The organizations need to increase activities, and a content activity has been raised a number of issues (Richard et. al., 2001; Tarafdar & Zhang, 2008; Zhou & DeSantis, 2005):

- **Bottlenecks**: sometimes the content have arrives in different form and edited manually into a suitable form in order to publishing on the website this process can lead to delays in publishing on the web.

- **Consistency**: web editing is developed to serve there can be inconsistency in the web look to the users who can be make feel the site and variable quality of design and content. In the beginning the company can losing the coherence of the style and design in it project, at the end may lead effect on the exploitation of a site's strategic value (Chenet. al., 2013).

- **Navigation**: are Uncensored, poorly usability can lead navigation and search capabilities making it hardly for content users to find information easily.

- **Data duplication**: The Web content is often a copy of data held in an administrative system, preferably, data will not be stored in duplicate in the organization. There will be one source accessed by all business applications.Where data needs to be copied then replication should be automated and controlled.

- **Content examination and control**: may published on the Web site unauthorized content, if the information acceptable from a marketing viewpoint? A legal viewpoint? Procedures and controls need to be defined to manage by Web publishing process.

*Tracking:** To use content effectively it is necessary to know everything about the information content, such as when and who is created website and last updated. The ability to monitoring and reconstruct the changes that have occurred to content management.

*Commercial Operations**: Content is often joined closely with Commercial Operations. For example, the production of a market information report is a complex Commercial Operations, involving data collection, data analysis, and the generation of explanation and forecasts. Also updates and modification are likely to be needed on a regular basis. The Commercial Operations and Web content management need to be integrated, allowing content to be published internally for investigation and review and only released once it has been approved. Furthermore, the process itself may need to be redesigned to take account of differences between paper and Web publishing.

Content management presents a significant challenge for each organization that provides information to customers, employees, salesmen and commercial partners. It also plays a vital role in the organization, classification and formation of informative resources, so that they can be stored, edited, published and deleted, depending on users' needs (Hackos, 2002; Connell, 2008).

Web Content Management WCM is a process of collecting data and information that allow people to create content or embellish it, using existing sources (Russell O'Hare, 2015). In order to store the content, it has to be converted into data that can be easily processed. The data, in turn, have to be structured and labeled with corresponding metadata (a dataset which describes and gives information about other data). Thus metadata supports processing of information by the computer (Mican et. al., 2009; McDermott, 2008).

Content Management System CMS- manages the content within the website. The content can be simple text, documents, video, photos, music or any other elements presented electronically (Fig 2.1). The main advantage of using content management system is that it does not require from users much technical knowledge to create or manage www content("What is Joomla?," 2015;Shariff, 2010; Goodwin et. al., 2006).

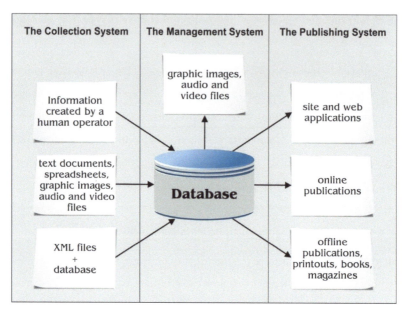

Fig. 2.1.The structure of a Web CMS, Schematic representation adapted from.

Source: B. Boiko, "Content Management Bible", 2 edition, Wiley, 2005.

The system responsible for web content management must allow for easy access tocontent components regardless of where and how they are stored (Richard et. al.,2001; Isa, 2009). They can be gathered in different structures, various types of databases (e.g. relational and object-oriented) or stored e.g. in file systems. To provide users with an efficient access to the web content, aspects related to information architecture design and websites usability should be taken into consideration, when creating websites (Ndou, 2004; Rosenfeld& Morville, 2002).

WCM system is fruitful when the business requires frequent updates to the content on the website/portal. What this means is, a business that needs to keep on updating its business information displayed on its websites to ensure that the website users can view the most up-to-date information available at a given point of time is a good candidate for a WCM.An online shopping website uploads its product information such as product descriptions, product images, price, and stock availability details etc. The information needs to be update. The stock information, if not updated on the site, would result in purchase orders for a product that is not available in the shop(Kathuria, 2006).

Instead of updating the website's HTML/JSP pages manually on a daily/weekly basis,the online shopping website firm can manage it effectively through a WCM system. Latest content information can be updated through the WCM content authoring tool and new product information can be easily entered without requiring any knowledge of web scripting tools(Kathuria, 2006; McKeever, 2003).

When creating a new project or editing the web project settings, you will notice the list of all of the available web forms. Basically, the forms that are defined in "Company Home Data Dictionary" Web Forms are available to the entire web projects along with templates and workflows associated with those forms (Netergistry,2014). Microsoft content management server MCMS provided a rich framework but at the same time required a significant amount of repetitive custom code to achieve core web content management WCM functionality such as site navigation and content aggregation (Shariff, 2010).

The website manager is responsible for the smooth functioning of the website. It is a software system that provideswebsiteauthoring, collaboration, and administration tools designed to allow users with little knowledge of webprogramminglanguagesormarkuplanguagesto create and manage website content with relative ease. The robust of WCM System can be provided the foundation for communications, and can supplying the users the abilities to manage documents and output for multiple author editing and participation(Johnston, 2013).

On a basic level it will offer such features as: easy content editing, versioning (revisions of your content), media management, workflow management for content publishing and approvals, modification template and a usable to use control of sorts to providing us an overview of site(s). Content management is a process of getting organized about creating your publications(Boiko, 2005).

It make users abilities to visit websites which have dynamic growing need through providing better design for brand and generate business. The information technology is become more effective with people with using mobile phone, which make them shopping and Marketing faster and easiest, the interactivity on the website is need to be adaptive and provide a seamless experience across platforms and devices. Meeting needs of content the web developers, designers, marketers and Entrepreneurs. Powerful info-structure can create experience through communication points and platform. The good strategy in online marketing can make more reliability and Authenticity to the users. Responsive design ensures and make the web pages much more consistent regardless of the device being used (Ted & Stephen, 2015).

The following list was chosen to reflect the Website development (Johnson-Eilola, 2002; Sammons, 2004; Summers &Michael, 2005).The list also reflects concerns addressed toWeb development and e-commerce:

Management and development content website (e.g., understanding of how to decide and what content including website, discussions people analysis and issues discriminating website.

- Organization and website structure (e.g., content interdependencyduetohyperlinks, structure of hierarchical).

- Strategies of visual design (e.g., effective and appropriate use of background, fonts, colors).

- Challenges facing developers of sites (i.e., "how to" Web- authoring tools, issues such as use of HTML).

- Technical issues influencing users and therefore will influence strategies usedon developers Websites (e.g., size of graphics files can influencing on a site's download time).

- Issues related with Website development process (e.g., team for development website; Outsourcing to develop the sites, testing usability).

Website manager should have a clear view of direction for its website and an overview about the important aspects of policy that might confirm this. At the current time the Government goals are more focused on transactional services. It is also important to ensure that the website reflects local priorities and a wide view about its participation. Encouraging take-up and usage is equally, if not more important than, adding new ever more sophisticated facilities(Kim & Lee, 2012). The key to effective website management is thedevelopment and implementation of a strategy designed toensure that it remains focused on what the organisation isthere to deliver as well as on what information and servicesthe target audiences expect to be able to access.For the website to be effective, anyone in the organisationshould be able to access the policy documents(UK e-Government Unit, 2003). These shouldcontain clear strategy aims:

- a description of what the website will deliver,

- publishing and business procedures,

- policy on achieving online transaction targets,

- policy on how the web, call centres and othercommunication and service channels will support eachother,

- corporate design and editorial style guides,

- guidelines on website navigation,

- advice on how pages, content and links are to be ownedand updated,

- guidelines on when to use .pdf files,

- advice on when and how to meet the needs of peoplewho need content in languages other thanEnglish,

- policy on meeting the terms of the Freedom ofInformation Act,

- policy on data protection and privacy,

- policy on disabled access to the site and meeting web accessibility initiative (WAI) recommendations,

- plans for user testing, and the ongoing results of thosetests,

- plans to develop the website in line with the results ofuser tests.

Some parts of the role of the central website teammay vary according to theorganization.There can be little doubt that one key function is the management ofwebsitestandards.Standards apply in four areas as illustrated by Figure 2.2 below.

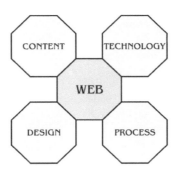

Fig. 2.2.Standards for website.
Source: Own elaboration.

The content and its properties (metadata) in the system need to be published out to the website so that it can be displayed on the site. Site Caching Services (SCS), formerly known as Web Cache, that helps us publish content and its metadata (document attributes) from Web Publisher system to a website, ensuring that the content seen on the website is accurate(Kathuria, 2006).

2.2   Information architecture and usability of websites

Since the mid-1990s, information and communications technology (ICT) have raised to the forefront of discussions related to globalization and development (economic, sustainable, or human). A citizen centric approach has fundamental consequences of the use of ICT in governance processes. As shown in Figure 2.3, citizens are both "clients" and "stakeholders" in the overall process (Zambrano, 2009; Weerakkody & Vishanth, 2009). Figure 2.3 showsE-governance framework "Dual role of citizens in e-governance".

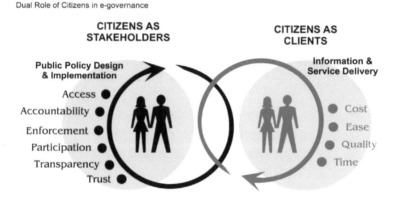

Fig. 2.3. E-governance framework "Dual role of citizens in e-governance",

Source:Weerakkody, Vishanth, ed.Social and Organizational Developments through Emerging E-Government Applications: New Principles and Concepts: New Principles and Concepts. IGI Global, 2009.p99

The difference between a website with no visitors from the search engines and a website that is full of visitors from the search engines is optimization. Search Engine Optimization is the difference between loss and profit on the Internet in the local government website(Jamak et. al.,2011; Nermend et. al., 2013).An accessible website is the one which makes no obstacles for users to access its contents. It provides full-value information to anyone independently from their abilities. This feature is essential for all websites, and multiply more for the public administration, and therefore, accessibility studies are carried out to examine these sites independently (Kopackova et. al.,2010). By investigating citizens and businesses and their service needs it may be possible to add knowledge on their impacts. It seems difficult to suggest improved products and services without knowing what the users really want from alocal government website system. To address this issue and provide a comprehensive understanding of user needs in terms of LGU website, it is a need of an increased research focus on user involvement in LGU website initiatives (Flak et. al., 2003).

There are two types of factor that influence take-up. The **first** set of factors is referred to as Necessary Conditions. Without these Necessary Conditions, services are unlikely to be much used, but they only work up to a threshold. Thus, people will not share sensitive information with the public sector unless they are comfortable about the security of their connection; once they are comfortable, further efforts to improve security will have little impact on take-up (Kolsaker& Lee-Kelley,2008).

The **second** set of factors is referred to as potential drivers. These are factors that are keys to achieving high take-up. When the right necessary conditions are in place, these Potential Drivers take over to determine usage. Thus, to extend the previous example, once users are comfortable about the security of their connection and other similar factors, they will only make the odd transaction. However if they understand, the financial advantage to using local government websites, and use more intensely multiple advantage and take-up will grow substantially(Lowe, 2003).

- **Information Architecture IA**

Information architecture (IA) is a science and an art of design of websites to support their usability, provide the easiest method to browse webpage content. An information architecture IA strategy is based on a conceptual framework for structuring and organizing a website. Thus this concept includes design of www navigation, structure, and links between particular webpages as well as design of information hierarchy on the individual pages (Morville, 2006).

Information architecture provides also that structure and layout of webpages is consistent and expectable on all webpages(Sharlin et. al., 2009).It involves steps such as evaluation of existing and needed content, layout of webpages, providing clues to help use the site efficiently, and developing navigational structure(Nowakowski, 2014).Information architecture considers importance of individual information on the webpage, enforces prioritization of published content. This is vital to both users and search engines(Dover & Dafforn, 2011).This refers in particular to extensive websites where mass information is published. Fig 2.4presents the general concept of information architecture including basic concepts and associated issues.

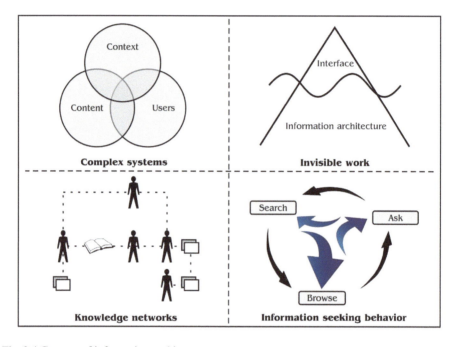

Fig. 2.4.Concept of information architecture.
Source: Morville P., Information Architecture on the World Wide Web, Handbook ISBN: 1-56592-282-4, First Edition, February 1998, P13.

Common information architecture is vital to ensuring that information and data can flow across government to provide seamless, efficient, secure and trusted services. It provides opportunities for the reuse of public data, benefiting the economy and fuelling innovation. The public sector information architecture will also consider how the public sector should manage its information: for example, will the public sector hold multiple copies of information or will it be held centrally and accessed by many? This has implications for all of the strands within the ICT Strategy, particularly data center rationalization, the Government Cloud and information assurance and security. It also affects decisions core to the Public Sector Network as it will impact on bandwidth requirements and likely volumes of data transfer (Smith, 2010).

Study can define the information architect as: 1) people who organizing the original patterns in data, can be make it more complicated; 2) developer who creates the map of information and structure which can allows others to find their individual paths to knowledge; 3) In the emerging 21st century professional can be addressing the needs of the age focused upon clarity, human perception and science of the organization of information. Structure and organizationare about building rooms. Navigation design is about adding doors and windows(Morville, 2006).

A fundamental problem for anyone wishing to engage with concepts of IA is the lack of a clear definition of its scope. This scope can be defined as(Nowakowski, 2014):

- classification and structure of websites, the structural design of shared information environments,
- ways of organizing information, the art and science of organizing,
- ways of naming (labeling), and labeling websites,
- use of navigation systems,
- use of information searching models,
- use of thesauri,
- controlled vocabularies and metadata,
- information architecture and graphic design for web,
- methods and techniques to study users of information,
- methods, criteria and indicators for evaluating the quality of network resources,
- intranets, online communities, and software to support usability and fundability.
- an emerging community of practice focused on bringing principles of design and architecture to the digital landscape (Batley, 2007).

The interconnections between people and content that underpin knowledge networks,and explain how these concepts can be applied to transform static web sites intocomplex adaptive systems is presented in Figure 2.5(Morville, 1998).

The information architecture itself contains what information should be collected from reviewer and displayed.

Much of the literature on information architecture examines content but restricts its coverage to high level content, dealing primarily with the information audit and with the organization and design of systems, back to IA being synonymous with taxonomy. This is a top-down approach to system content representing an ideal (Batley, 2007). Studymustbe prepared to going deeply into detail, identifying and defining the component systems that support our sites. Figure 2.5shows how semantic networks canprovide a foundation for easy navigation. And the study must convince that an effective searching experience requires not just a good engine or anice interface, but a carefully integrated system of interdependent parts(Morville, 2006).

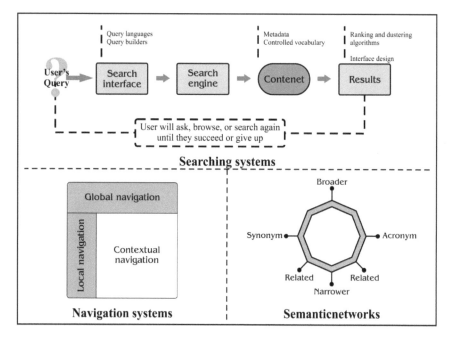

Fig. 2.5.Information architecture systems.

Source: Morville P." Information Architecture on the World Wide Web", Handbook, First Edition, 1998, p14.

Content analysis and content mapping are part of the information architecture development process. They will influence basic functionality, i.e. software applications, and taxonomy creation. Continuing usability of the system presupposes strategies for managing the content. As stated previously, no matter how well designed the system, no matter how elegant and robust the architecture is, the system is only going to be of benefit if it includes all the documentation and information its users need. That presupposes that the information and documentation is effectively managed.

An information system stores, organizes and provides access to content. The information system has architecture. These concepts are, therefore, inter-related, and an analysis of content management can be usefully developed within the context of general aspects of information systems and information architecture (Batley, 2007).

Information architecture emphasizes the combination of science and art of information expression, focuses on providing the content of information to users in a clear, transparent and easy-to-use way.IA and usability share the same target, have relationship in their nature and complement each other.

Government websites often have information of different types and of large quantities, as well as are of interest of different users. Usability of such websites should be one of the important aspects of their creation process. So the theory and method of information architecture could take effects over the entire LGU websites lifespan(Zhou, 2009).It should be ensured that strategy of information architecture is understandable and accepted by website designers, programmers, content managers and any other entities and people involved in design, creation and management of a website Achieving the optimum information architecture is one of the main objectives to obey usability principles in websites design processes.

Usability means that people who use a system can do so quickly and easily to accomplish their own tasks. Even though a system may perform well by other measures, without satisfactory usability a system is not successful because it does not meet the users' needs (Cao et. al.,2004). Users should be able to use a configuration intuitively and experience success in doing so.For example, the configuration process should be coherently structured along clear navigation paths (Streichsbier et. al., 2009).Thus usability ensures users to achieve specified goals with effectiveness, efficiency and satisfaction in a specified context of use. It means the accuracy and completeness with which users achieve specified goals (effectiveness), the resources expended to increase the accuracy with which users achieved goals efficiency, acceptability and comfort of use (satisfaction),(Wang, 2011; Szewczyk, 2014).Usability refers to:

Usability according to Nielsen (1993) includes the following issues:

- learnability, which describes the ease to learn the functionality of the system, what means how soon a user who has never before entered www is able to accomplish basic tasks on this website,

- efficiency, which refers to the level of performance, user's accessibility to certain system components, promptness of learning interface and performance of certain tasks in already known system,

- memorability, what means the ease of remembering the system functionality, so that one can recall how to use system after period of non-using,

- few errors relate to capability of the system to feature a low error rate, to support users making few errors during the use of the system, and in case they make errors, to help them to easy recover,

- user's satisfaction is a measure according to which the user finds the system friendly in use, so this measure defines to what extent a user is satisfied with the website (Nielsen, 1993).

Some factors may influence Websites usability. These may be e.g.: language version, and in fact a method for creating webpages for users coming from different countries. Originally the Internet was dominated by English therefore commonly accepted standards of www usability also follow standards suited to English websites. However in the early twenty-first century, the growth of international Internet users has reached the amount where non-English speakers are much more than English speakers(Makki & Leppert, 2006).The most popular languages on the Internet to date is: English, Chinese, Spanish, Arabic, Japanese, French, Portuguese, German, Russian and Korean. However, despite the variety of languages being used on the Internet currently, the web is still designed to handle English input and output (Rand, 2012), evident by the fact that all web scripting languages are based on English.

A majority of multicultural web usability research suggests creating separated versions of the same website for other regions, also known as localization. Observing local industry style of the targeted culture is a recommended method for planning a localized design (Reinecke & Bernstein, 2013). Designers with matching cultural background are most likely to produce better localized web sites, for the cultural norms that they include into the design will most likely be more accurately reflecting the targeted culture than a foreign designer, even if the inclusion is not intentional (Nacar & Burnaz, 2011).

According to Nielsen, The study used for (flexibility, user-satisfaction, and few errors) to test usability for each LGU website, this process done through make the users using free to evaluate each LGU website during examination each website in web tracking system. The system is allow the users assessment each website according FUF using likert scale from 0..9 (Kallas, 2011). The first parameter (flexibility) is including Learnability, Efficiency, and Memorability. The second and third parameter is the same criteria which has been mentioned in the Nielsen research.

Usability test (also called Usability testing) is one of the most popular methods of utility assessment, based largely on the approach to user-oriented design (UCD – User-centered design). This method is used primarily to evaluate the functionality and usability of websites. Usability testing has mostly taken the form of laboratory tests in which testers perform tasks that simulate user interaction with the website and specially adapted computer workstations. Usability testing, unlike the group of tests, is carried out usually on individual users and relies on the practical use of some of service features. During the performance of specific tasks, participants are asked to pay attention to what they see, do and feel and then describe their experience verbally or in writing(Nowakowski, 2014; Hom, 1998).

Usability tests are used to measure usability of webpage or application, are currently carried out through IT tools. These can include: an electronic poll form (to collect user's opinion), user activity recording software or tools for tracking user's activity (use of links), time spent on the individual sites. The most common areas of activity of the analysed websites refer to the following aspects: visibility of navigation, clarity and legibility of icons and ease to find required information (James, 2008).

Usability testing is an irreplaceable usability practice since it provides a direct input on how real users use the system. Participants in testing are real user of the product and their responses are representative of views and opinions of the customers. During tests the participants use the prototype or product according to given instructions. These activities aim to help to fix out the problems existing in the product, or to give instructions to design a new product(Wang, 2011).

Usability testing is related to tasks associated with browsing and general site navigation, purchasing goods and services or submitting data via forms. Usability tests are relating to research on effectiveness of a specific solution, ease to remember, ease to learn, subjective error tolerance by users(Al-Badi & Mayhew, 2010).Accordingly, if the conceptual model is coherent to the users, it will result in an appropriate mental model in the user's mind, and finally enhance the webpage usability. The government website should consider the needs of users in order to be coherent to the users' mental model(Kim et. al.,2007; Alshaaliet. al.,2011).

The usability of an information webpage evaluated by the basis of usability set attribute measures. This assessment conducted with any level in the lifecycle of webpage development by having users use the webpage to perform certain tasks (pre-specified or unlimited). The goal of the assessment is to not only assess the webpage usability but also provide guidelines for improving the usability and entire website quality. In the early levels of WebPages development, designers of the websites can use a formative evaluation to test the detailed aspects of the information system design and correct the design based on the evaluation results. This is often a reduplicate process. Next the website has been developed, designers may use summative evaluation to determine the usability of the achievable website. Researchers can evaluate a single webpage, or conduct controlled experiments to compare the usability of the system developed to alternative existing WebPages with similar working (Cao et. al.,2004).

The accessibility of websites is frequently referred to together with usability. The website should be accessible for visually-impaired people, blind people, people who have problems with moving their hands and also for mobile devices and Internet search engines. Should accessibility and usability be combined? Certain elements of websites, e.g. which make them more accessible for the disabled, have an impact on their widely understood usability; for instance, contrast between letters and background. If it is not clear, accessibility and usability will be subject to deterioration. Nevertheless, such a situation is observed relatively seldom; hence greater accessibility does not always entail greater usability. Thus, it may be concluded that in some aspects accessibility is a subset of usability, yet this is not a general rule. Even a website that is perfectly adjusted to screen readers used by blind people may be hardly usable for all the users. Other people may not notice these efforts. Nevertheless, limited accessibility does not immediately translate into reduced usability, e.g. when blind and visually-impaired people are not the target group of a particular project (Rek et. al.,2011). Experts in usability state that the first two seconds after entering a given website and the impressions received after this time are strategic. It is then that they may leave the website and not want to enter it again. In fact, this is not surprising as a user experience (UX), i.e. all impressions that he/she has gained while using an interactive product should be as positive as possible. How to achieve this? A solution is a proper design of interaction so that the product is attractive, functional and ergonomic, and the user is satisfied and content with using it. The UX is a basis for usability that involves the following three key areas relating to the ergonomics of a website, namely:

- intuitive navigation,

- facilitating the scan in search for information,

- providing communication comprehensible for the user (Kaushik, 2009).

This seems clear and obvious, yet practice shows that authors often mess around and their "ego"or lack of knowledge make them develop websites that do not satisfy users' needs.

The contribution of design disciplines to the realization of usable websites seems indisputable. However, so called designed websites still show shortcomings with respect to appreciation, accessibility, and informative content. A wide range of performance and usability measurement methods exist. Only a few support the mapping of how human beings perceive and value a site. Most usability techniques are quantitative and measure the performance, retrieval times, and success times/failure rates. Qualitative assessments usually consist of observations and interviews. In short a typical repertory grid session consists of the following steps (Verlinden & Coenders, 2000):

Step 1: Eliciting constructs. Each construct consists of a likeness and contrast pole (study refer to these as "dimensions").

Step 2: Indexing elements on these constructs.

Step 3: Quantification of the perceptions of end users through rating, ranking and/or sorting of elements.

Step 4: Statistical analysis to find out about element distance, construct centrality, and preferences.

In order to conduct our research, analyze a few factors namely: screen appearance, consistency, accessibility, navigation, media use, interactivity and content. The seven factors are explained below: screen appearance would indicate the design of the website in terms of the on-screen information, consistency refers to the uniformity of design, taking into considerations graphics, placement and observable schemes and patterns, web accessibility would refer the ability to access the web site from different browser platforms, either software or hardware related, navigation would take into consideration the "hyper-movements" between pages and between websites, media use refers to the use of multimedia i.e., text, graphics, video, animation, etc., interactivity refers to the level of communication of the website in the form of contact information, enquiries, forum and so on, content refers to the information and general gist of the website (Teohet. al., 2009).

The usability and accessibility must be considered together when some web content is created and published, but that the responsibility of guaranteeing them must not be assigned to people who are neither expert in computer technologies nor in usability and accessibility. This responsibility must be assigned to the system, which must properly support its users in creating and publishing accessible and usable web pages (Fogli et. al., 2010).

As far as Poland is concerned, it is still widely discussed which is the best translation of the term "**usability**". There are two schools of thought. The first one, presented mainly in the literature, uses the word "**functionality**", the second one – "**usability**". The latter seems to be a better choice. In English "functionality" determines the number of functions that satisfy user's needs, whereas "usability" defines how easy it is to understand and use these functions. This is a very clear and comprehensive definition. However, it is not that easy to translate it into Polish. According to a number of dictionaries, functionality is a synonym of usability. Nevertheless, in the field of IT, these two terms are used in line with their English equivalents (Szewczyk, 2014).

The aim of usability testing of LGU webpages is not only the evaluation of usability of the existing www but obtaining guidelines for a new webpage design. Research should refer not only to a single website, but also similar systems to verify usability of proposed solutions (Cao et. al., 2004). There are growing interests of research of usability measurement in website (Rahim et. al., 2009; Rahim et. al., 2010). The usability measures are being measured by using Nielson usability guideline for the uploading speed and page size of the main page and number of broken links (Nielsen, 2000).

The popularity of websites including LGU websites is directly connected with their quality, usability, with what type of information can be obtained and how a user can navigate such a website. The study of LGU sites quality ought to be a regular feature in their development, especially since the results of such study can be provided as guidelines for designers of such websites. The guidelines may regard modification and development of LGU sites so that they are consistent with the needs of users which are often difficult and not evident to describe. Quality of LGU website and users' evaluation can be and often are responsible for website's popularity and frequency of visit. The reference books on this matter describe many methods and models of evaluation which, however, in most cases are based on data obtained in the form of surveys. The practical methods of data collecting can be divided into three groups:

- using survey and questionnaire,

- based on expert's opinion,

- using analysis of user traces.

Surveys and questionnaires are used to get users' opinions on websites and on evaluation of selected quality criteria. It is an easy way to collect relevant data based on simple structure of a survey and possibility to file it on the Internet. Collected data is later analysed using one of many methods of evaluation of website quality and final result is an average grade of the site (Parlaketal, 2008).

Method of expert's opinion is based on using an expert or a group of experts in the certain field for evaluation. Usually, an individual expert analyses and provides evaluation of the entire website considering many criteria but he can also evaluate individual elements of the site (Seock, 2007). In case evaluation is performed by a group of experts it is based on the opinion of each expert (regarding the entire site of some of its elements) (Chmielarz, 2008).The final grade is usually the result of experts' discussion(Chmielarz, 2008a).This method is most widely used with websites which have measurable features. An example can be e-commerce. In case of websites with clear qualitative features (news sites, internet portals, LGU sites) the method is not a good solution.

Analysis of user traces is mainly employed for testing usability of websites. The research includes analysis of user's behavior during website navigation. The easiest solution in this group of methods is supervision by an observer of user navigation and manner of access to relevant data. The observer follows user's navigation and user's paths to find relevant information as well as monitors time needed and user's reaction to the site's responses. As a result of this process a document which allows verifying the correctness of each website within a web-portal is produced (Holzinger, 2005).

More advanced methods of user trace analysis, which require use of additional equipment and software, are called eyetracking (Nielsen& Pernice, 2010).All models of evaluation of website quality use many dimensions of quality description. However, they differ in dimension, its structure and quantity. Criteria used for evaluation of quality can be grouped thematically (hierarchical structure) or they can be set on one level. These criteria depend on type of website for which a model is made. The importance of each dimension can be analysed in two categories. The first one requires user gradation of each part of website, the second one sets each part a-priori on the same level.

When analysing the most popular models of website evaluation, the following ones must be highlighted:

- Website Quality Model.
- SERVQUAL i e-SERVQUAL.
- SITEQUAL.
- E-SEQUAL.
- WAES.
- eQual.

- **Website Quality Model**

This model was based on the model of quality Kano which defined three levels of client expectations towards the quality of the product or service. The first level (termed basic) defines factors which, if non-existent, cause dissatisfaction with the product. However, if they do exist, it still does not mean that clients are satisfied (Morrisonet. al., 2005). Therefore, these factors are the most basic ones which should be included in every product or service. The second level (termed performance) defines those elements of the product which allow it to be made distinct from other similar products or services. The third level (termed exciting) defines those elements which make the product one step ahead of the client and ensure proper level of excitement and client's loyalty towards the provider(Zhang et. al., 2001).

Eleven primary criteria of website evaluation and forty-two criteria for each category have been defined by WQM model research. The following are part of primary criteria: information content, cognitive outcome, pleasure of use, privacy, possibility

/power given to user, appearance, technical support, navigation, organisation of information, credibility, objectivity(Zhang & von Dran, 2002).

This model is used in quality evaluation of various websites, it does not provide a formalised methodology or research.

SERVQUAL and e-SERVQUAL.E-SERQUAL model is derived from the SERQUAL model of research and evaluation of service quality. SERQUAL model is used for evaluation of the difference between actual and desired quality of service. It defines five criteria of quality (integrity, reliability, provider responsibility, certainty, accessibility) and a grade is created based on a survey of twenty-two questions(Parasuraman et. al., 1988). The survey uses a seven degree scale to describe one's expectations towards quality of service and it also describes the current quality of service.

E-SERQUAL model is the adaptation of SERQUEL scale for the need to evaluate internet service quality. This model retains some of the criteria and adds more (quality of internet service)(Zeithaml et. al., 2002).

This model is subdivided into two different models: four-criterion E-S-QUAL (efficiency, fulfilment of promise, system availability, privacy) and three-criterion E-RecS-QUAL (provider responsibility, compensation, contact). Figures for criteria of the model E-S-QUAL are obtained from a survey containing twenty-two statements describing service quality whereas figures for criteria of the model E-RecS-QUAL are obtained from a survey containing eleven questions(Parasuraman et. al. , 2005). This model is designed for evaluation of websites which offer services, e.g. e-commerce, auction websites, internet banking etc. However, it is not designed for evaluation of information websites.

SITEQUAL is mainly used for evaluation of online shops. At first, it included nine dimensions of quality evaluation which were grouped into two categories. The first category included criteria connected with sale and the second category included criteria connected with website quality. As a result of further research on the model, it was decided to leave only four criteria (how easy it is to use, quality of appearance/project, and rate of processing, safety). Furthermore, a nine-question survey is used in the research(Yoo & Donthu, 2001).

E-SEQUAL, similar to SITEQUAL, is a method of evaluating the quality of online shops. It is used in expert evaluation. It includes defined heuristics of human-website interaction and management of customer relation.These are the following: pre-shopping steps of interaction, interaction during shopping and post-shopping interaction(Minocha et. at., 2004).

WAES (Website Attribute Evaluation System) is a model dedicated to evaluation of local government websites. In this model there are two groups of criteria (regarding transparency and interactivity). Each group includes five criteria which, in turn, include a number of sub-criteria. In total, there are c. forty criteria which evaluate website quality. Binary value is used for evaluation (Pawlowskaet. at.,2013).Value 1 when the feature is included in the website and is correct, value 0 when the feature is not present(Wanget. al.,2005).

EQUAL was created on the base of WebEQualmodel which used the Quality Function Deployment. This function provided method of identification and introduction of user opinion on product quality at subsequent levels. At first, the model defined twenty-four survey questions which corresponded to 8 criteria grouped into four categories (Barnes & Vidgen, 2000). The next version of eQual model used criteria connected with user-website interaction from SERQUAL model(Barnes & Vidgen, 2005). Subsequent version modified groups of criteria and changed survey questions which resulted in a list of twenty-two statements (sub-criteria) and five criteria grouped into three categories(Barnes & Vidgen, 2006). Currently, eQual model is the best formalised model of evaluation of website quality.

When studying models of evaluation of website quality presented in literature, one may notice that the majority of them are used for evaluation of a certain type of websites. There are models for evaluation of e-commerce but not so many models which can be applied for LGU website evaluation.

The importance of the problem of website quality evaluation, as well as research on usability of websites, is reflected in the results of research conducted in Poland and publications of Polish scholars (Kowalczyk, 2000).

One of the authors who noticed the problem of website quality evaluation and the need to research it is WitoldChmielarz. In his works and conference papers he discussed various methods of evaluation of websites including local government websites

(Chmielarz, 2008; Chmielarz et. al., 2008; Chmielarz et. al.,2011; Chmielarz, 2013).Also, MarcinSikorski, the author of many academic papers and books on user-system interaction and quality of IT systems, research has been done on ergonomics of interactive systems (websites) (Sikorski, 2002; Sikorski, 2009; Sikorski, 2010; Sikorski, 2012). The subject literature also includes numerous publications on website quality by Budziński's R. team Ziemba P., Piwowarski M., Jankowski J.,Wątróbski J.,(Ziemba& Budziński, 2011; Ziemba & Budziński, 2010; Ziemba& Piwowarski, 2010; Ziemba, 2013; Ziembaet. al.,2014).

The problem of website design (corporate portals) and implementation of these solutions in LGU was researched by ZiembaE. And her team(Ziemba, 2005; Ziemba, 2009; Ziemba et. al.,2014).Evaluation of website usability, research on methods of implementation are also present in numerous publications, e.g. Fabisiak L. (Fabisiak & Wolski, 2010; Fabisiak, 2012; Fabisiak, 2013), Czerwinski A. and Krzesaj M. (Czerwiński & Krzesaj, 2014), Karwatka T.(Karwatka, 2009) or KasperskiM.(Kasperski & Boguska-Torbicz, 2008).

2.3   Research methods for website usability

Testing websitesusability includes series of methods, techniques or tools to measure and evaluate ease and effectiveness of a website by a user and general user satisfaction. The most important methods to evaluate usability of a website are the inspection methods and the user test methods.

The inspection methods such as the heuristic evaluation or cognitive walkthrough, under subjective evaluation of user's usability, help to define the usability problems. The evaluation is performed by experts in the field. They use their expertise and try to detect potentially negative situations. The product of their work is a report including problems found and suggested solutions. Detected problems should be verified by user tests (Banati et. al.,2006). The user test methods employ techniques to collect data from the representative group of users who are to perform tasks defined in scenarios. Activities performed by the tested users are monitored by a person acting as a moderator or are recorded. These can be either formal in nature, where actual experiments are conducted to accept/reject a hypothesis or an iterative cycle of tests can be conducted to identify the usability deficiencies and gradually improve the concerned product (Rubin & Dana, 2004). The cost of user tests is considerably high because it should include the larger users' group.

Both methods have their advantages and disadvantages. An effective usability process should ideally combine the inspection and user testing methods, despite the fact that they evaluate usability independently. In general, there are number of methods used in website evaluation (Shneiderman, 1997; Jati, 2010). The general overview of these methods is presented in Table 2.1.

Table 2.1.Variety of expert-review methods for website evaluation.

Expert-review method	Explanation
Heuristic evaluation	Evaluators critique the design by conforming with a list of consisting usability elements.
Review and guide-lines	Evaluator follows organizational checklists or other well known guide-lines. This may take a long time for evaluation.
Consistency inspec-tion	The purpose of a consistency inspection is to check the extent of the consistency of the website elements such as color, fonts, output forms, consistency of terminology etc.
Cognitive walkthrough	Evaluators stimulate users navigating a website to conduct certain tasks to identify errors in website's interface.
Formal usability in-spection	The reviewer holds a formal meeting with a website design team to present the interface and to discuss its merits and weaknesses. This type requires a great deal of time for preparation.

Source: Horan,et. al., - Assessing user satisfaction of e-government services: development and testing of quality-in-use satisfaction with advanced traveler information systems (ATIS). . IEEE, Vol. 4, pp. 83b-83b, 2006.

Heuristic evaluation

This type of heuristic evaluationcan find usability problems more cost-effectively than other evaluation methods. The heuristic evaluation is inexpensive compared to oth-er evaluation methods (Nielsen, 2000; Tanet. al., 2009).An evaluator skilled in practical use of this method, without necessary involvement of representative users, can produce high quality results in the limited time(Kantner & Rosenbaum, 1997).In principle, heu-ristic evaluation can be conducted by only one evaluator.

In performing a heuristic evaluation, each evaluator steps through the interface twice. First, to get a general idea about the general scope of the system and its navigation structure.Second, to focus on the screen layout and interaction structure in more detail, evaluating their design and implementation against the predefined heuristics. Each heuristic evaluation results in a list of usability flaws with reference to the heuristic violated. After the problems are found, preferably each evaluator independently estimates the severity of each problem(Jaspers, 2009). Heuristic evaluation is an efficient usability evaluation method (Jeffries & Heather, 1992) with a high benefit–cost ratio(Nielsen, 1994).

Use of heuristic evaluation in testing usability seem to be more helpful than presented by Nielsen (1994), since the frame of research is described there and the specific functionality to be reviewed is mentioned. Table 2.2presents the main categories used in heuristic evaluation (Molich& Nielsen, 1990).

Table 2.2.Main Categories for Use in Heuristic Evaluations

No.	Categories
1	Visibility of system status - provide feedback, indicate progress, identify cues, etc.
2	Match between system and real world - speak the users, language, familiar terms, etc.
3	User control and freedom - obvious way to undo, make actions reversible, etc.
4	Consistency and standards - express same thing same way, uniformity, etc.
5	Error prevention - design system to prevent errors, identify cues, etc.
6	Recognition rather than recall - see-and-point instead of remember-and-tell, etc.
7	Flexibility and efficiency of use - user-interface customizable, shortcuts, etc.
8	Aesthetic and minimalist design
9	Helping users, recognize, diagnose, and recover from errors

Source: Nielsen J. Usability engineering.Elsevier, 1994.

The usability constructs to be more helpful thanNielsen's (1994), because they describe the construct, or the what, and identify specificfunctionality to review. If a novice reviewer used Table 2.2 as a guide for reviewing a website,they may not know where to look or how to determine whether error prevention, for example,was used or not.

In relation to the number of evaluators that find the most usability problems, suggested that "Four expert heuristic evaluators found more problems than any other evaluation technique, including usability testing". This result confirmed by three expert evaluators found more usability problems than were founded by other evaluation techniques found. Despite the fact that most evaluation techniques basically require experts in website usability subjects, heuristic evaluation can be carried out by evaluators with no formal usability training. However, evaluators who have information technology, for example computer programmers, can conduct the heuristic evaluation process (Abanumy, 2006).

User plays a pivotal role in success of all IS projects. Yet in the worldwide local government website seeks to provide successfully service, but have fallen short of their potential. Online transactions with public administrations are working extremely hard to avoid failure of the data protection and privacy resulting in unwillingness to participating inlocal government website. Although trust is confirmed to be an effective implement for dealing with the concern of the anonymous transactions, the majority of trust studies have been conducted in the context of e-commerce. Recently, several research has focused on the role of trust influencing willingness of citizens to use local government website services (Akkaya et. al.,2011).

The findings presented here are taken from the nationwide local government website survey, which has been conducted together with TNS (TNS is one of the most renowned institutions for market research and public opinion research in Germany). The study was carried out in June 2010. Interviews were conducted online with a nationwide representative sample of 1,002 internet users in private households by an online panel weighted by central features like gender, age and formal education (Cohenet. al.,2007). The study focuses on the local government website usage for the internet users of private households in Germany. Participants answered questions about the importance of local government website services, barriers to adoption of local government website, concerns of data security and privacy. The final sample comprised n=1,002 adults (46% female and 54% male) who are older than 18 years. Thirty-two percent (32%) are between the ages 18 to 34 years, forty-four percent (44%) are in the 35-54 age group and twenty-four percent (24%) of the sample are over the age 55. The importance of factors for using local government website services was measured on a five-point Likert-scale (1=least important to 5=crucial) and the barriers to adoption of local government website services were measured on a four-point Likert-scale (1=strongly disagree to 4=strongly agree) (Akkaya et. al.,2011).

Table 2.3 provides the results of study in which they conducted a review of the literature with the purpose of identifying various website usability constructs (for example, navigation, consistency, etc.), (Lee & Kozar, 2012). It also includes a list of related studies as well as question used to measure the construct. For example, for the construct *learnability*, one of the questions used to measure learnability is mean*"I can remember how to reach the same page I visited next time"*.

Table 2.3.The Constructs, Definitions, Related Studies, and Measurement Questions.

No.	Construct	Definition	Usability Measurement Question
1	Consistency	Consistent location of page components within and across pages	1) The website repeats the same structure, components, and overall looks across pages. 2) The website contains similar components across web pages. 3) Web pages in the website are consistently designed. 4) Each web page on the website is of similar design. 5) The website adheres to rules and standards of other online shopping sites.
2	Navigability	Capability to provide alternative interaction and navigating techniques	1) The website provides multiple search features (e.g., search engine, menu bar, go back-and-forward button, etc.) to obtain the target information. 2) The web page that I am looking for can be reached through multiple pathways. 3) There are multiple ways to access the web page that I am looking for and/or return to shopping menus. 4) It is very easy to locate what is needed in this website. 5) The website keeps the user oriented as they shop.
3	Supportability	Additional information and support mechanisms readily available to enhance the website use experience	1) While visiting the website, I feel that I can get just-in-time support anytime I need it. 2) The website provides features to ask for help anytime I need. 3) Getting support through a series of options is easy and convenient.

4	Learnability	Easy to learn the main functionality and gain proficiency to complete the tasks	1) The contents provided by the website are easily understood. 2) The website is designed for easy understanding. 3) I can easily remember how to reach the same page when I visit next time. 4) As time passes, I am more accustomed to the website with less effort.
5	Simplicity	Provision of minimum contents and functions within a website	1) The structure of the website is succinct. 2) I can comprehend most components of a page within seconds. 3) The website has components that are not necessary. 4) There are redundant components in the Website.
6	Interactivity	Website's ability to create vivid interaction and communication with users	1) The website provides an appropriate amount of interactive features (e.g., graphics, pop-up windows, animation, music, voices). 2) The website contains components to help the interaction between it and consumers. 3) Interactive features of the website are vivid and evoke responses. 4) The website provides features for interactive communication between consumers, or between consumers and the online company.
7	Readability	Extent to which website components are well organized and easy to read and understand	1) The website's wording is clear and easy to understand. 2) The website has enough white space (or margins) to make it readable. 3) Every page contains the appropriate amount of components to fit into a page. 4) The website uses colors and structures that are easy on the eyes.
8	Content relevance	Extent to which the content is up-to date and pertinent	1) The website contains in-depth information. 2) The website provides up-to-date information. 3) The scope of information provided by the website is appropriate. 4) The information provided by the website is accurate.

9	Credibility	A holistic concept that covers an online user's perception of security, privacy, and reliability during the navigation	1) I feel safe in my transactions with the website. 2) I trust the website to keep my personal information safe. 3) I trust the website administrators will not misuse my personal information. 4) The website is stable to use. 5) Services are routinely delivered as promised. 6) The website provides detailed information about security features.
10	Telepresence	Sense of presence in a virtual environment created by a computer/communication medium	1) I felt empathy with the website. 2) I feel I have personal ties to the website. 3) I feel as though I am emotionally connected to the website. 4) I feel as though I am taking part with the website.

Source: Lee Y.& Kozar K. A. Understanding of website usability: Specifying and measuring constructs and their relationships,Elsevier, Decision Support Systems, 52(2), 450-463, 2012, p454.

Table 2.4 indicate that each item took the form of a declarative statement suggesting whether needs were being met, or not, with respondents agreeing or disagreeing on a 7-point Likert-type scale. In this method, the author has been evaluated according 10 criteria, and obtained the answers for those people to give opinion about website as a part of process evaluate.

Table 2.4.Categories of Website Usability Testing

No.	Category	Description
1	Ease of use	Usability, accessibility, navigability, and logical structure
2	Responsiveness	Accessibility of service, e-mail service, reply to customer, contactinformation, and intuitive online help
3	Fulfillment	Order process, accuracy of service promise, billing accuracy, onlinebooking process, and confirmation, on-time delivery
4	Security/Privacy	Information protection, online purchase security, and privacy statement
5	Personalization	Individualized attention, customization of offerings and information
6	Visual appearance	Attract attention, convey image, and aesthetics

7	Information quality	Variety, scope, currency, conciseness, accuracy, authority, reliability,and uniqueness
8	Trust	Brand recognition, consistency, intentions, and credibility
9	Interactivity	Interactive features and communication (FAQs, guest books, chat)
10	Advertising/persuasion	Marketing, promotional content, suggested products, recom-mendation,and incentives
11	Playfulness	Enjoyment, fun, pleasure, and flow
12	Technology integration	New technology and integration

Source:Chiou Wen-Chih, Chin-Chao Lin, and ChyuanPerng. "A strategic framework for web-site evaluation based on a review of the literature from 1995–2006."Information & management47.5 (2010): pp282-290.p285

Tables 2.4 present the results of review of the literature to identify categories to test during website usability testing. These criteria are consolidated into twelve categories(Chiou et. al.,2010).Ease of use, information quality, responsiveness, visual appearance, security/privacy, interactivity, trust, fulfillment, personalization, advertising/persuasion, playfulness, and technology integration.The classification conducted a consensus process for assigning each study's proposed criteria into one of the 12 unified factors. Important factor influencing the efficiency of website usage is accessibility. The higher accessibility level of the government websites are, the more information will the people get from the websites. Therefore it will increase the efficiency of online business of government websites. The following methods can improve the current accessibility (Zhenxiang & Huaihe, 2010; Lazaret. al., 2004):

A. **Perfect the relevant laws**: From the experience of developed countries, study can get if the obstacle-free information wanted to be surely implemented, it must have strong laws as security. In developed countries, since 1990s or may be even earlier the concept of information barrier-free has caused the related people attention and has been carried out researches and the relevant regulations and standards have been formulated in the government-backed.

B. **Establishing and perfecting supervision mechanism**: supervision mechanism should be established and the test and evaluation of accessibility should be carried out regularly. And the results should be provided to the relevant departments as reference to modify the websites and the substandard ones should be punished according to the relevant laws.

C. **Provide information barrier-free construction funding**: The government at all levels shall establish special funds to safeguard information accessibility. Thesemechanisms can be top-down, namely the government first establish special funds, buy barrier-free detections and auxiliary equipment and train personnel to develop, manage and main their own websites to be barrier-free.

Another way of capturing information about user behavior is via an on-line questionnaire which can be used to capture technical, demographic, user satisfaction and/or visit information. One of the major concerns with on-line questionnaires, and indeed any form of feedback mechanism, is the self-selecting nature of the sample, raising concerns as to whether or not the users who have answered the questionnaire are typical users (Stieger & Reips, 2010). While there will always be concerns about the self-electing nature of the sample, if it can be shown that a large proportion of visitors to the site complete the questionnaire, and there are enough results to identify common trends in the answers, then an on-line questionnaire can provide useful information to the site developer. On-line questionnaires can help to build models of user behavior and track changes in that behavior over time. One technique which may prove more reliable for sites with search facilities is the analysis of search terms used (Stieger & Reips, 2010).

Previous research has shown that user frustration increases when page load times exceed 8 to 10 seconds of time without feedback (Bouch et. al.,2000).And approximately 60% of information searched on websites are not successfulwhich in turn leads to lower productivity, greater frustration experienced by the Internet user,loss of money (about 50% of losses is caused by the fact that the Internet user has not found theproduct he/she is seeking), probability of visiting a given website again (40% of users do not visita given website again because of the negative first impression) or loss of time experienced by users(Szewczyk, 2014).Usability of websites improves these statistics. Newer evidence shows that broadband users are less tolerant of web page delays than narrowband users, studyfound that 33% of broadband shoppers are unwilling to wait more than four seconds for a web page to load, whereas 43% of narrowband users will not wait more than six seconds.Speed is the second most important factor, after site attractiveness, to increasing flow in users (see Figure 2.6). People who are more engaged while browsing your site will learn faster and show an improved attitude and behavior toward your site. To increase perceived speed, strive to display your initial useful content in less than one or two seconds by layering and streamlining your content. Once total load time exceeds six to eight seconds, provide linear feedback to extend the tolerable wait time by lowering stress levels and allowing users to plan ahead (Akamai, 2006; Aliaset. al.,2011).

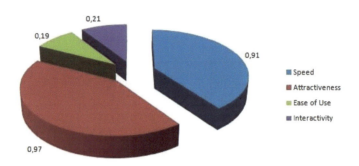

Fig. 2.6.Factors that affect flow in websites.
Source :KingA. B., " Website Optimization", O'Reilly Media, Inc. ISBN: 978-0-596-51508-9, Printed in the United States of America, 2008, pp1-349,P149.

Web page optimization streamlines your content to maximize display speed. Fast display speed is the key to success with your website (King, 2008). It increases profits, decreases costs, and improves customer satisfaction (not to mention search engine rankings, accessibility, and maintainability). To maximize web page display speed, you can employ the following 10 techniques: minimize HTTP requests, resize and optimize images, optimize multimedia, convert JavaScript behavior to code Cascading Style Sheets (CSS), use server-side sniffing, optimize JavaScript for execution speed and file size, convert table layout to code Cascading Style Sheets (CSS) layout, replace inline style with code Cascading Style Sheets (CSS) rules, minimize initial display time, and load JavaScript wisely(Szewczyk, 2014; Skulimowski, 2008).

The following tips are derived for High Performance Web Sites (King, 2008): make fewer HTTP requests to reduce object overhead, use a content delivery network, add an Expires header, gzip/compress text components, put style sheets at the top in the head, put scripts at the bottom of the body, avoid CSS expressions which are CPU-intensive and can be evaluated frequently, make JavaScript and CSS files external, reduce Domain Name System (DNS) lookups to reduce the overhead of DNSdelay by splitting lookups between two to four unique hostnames, minify JavaScript, avoid redirects which slow performance, remove duplicate scripts to eliminate extra HTTP requests in Internet Explorer.

Depending on the phase in which evaluation is performed, it is possibleto distinguish between formative evaluation, which takes place duringdesign, and summative evaluation, which takes place after the product hasbeen developed, or even when any prototype version is ready. During the nearly design stages the goal of the formative evaluation is to check thedesign team understanding of the users' requirements, and to test designchoices quickly and informally, thus providing feedback to the designactivities. Later on, the summative evaluation can support the detection ofusers' difficulties, and the improvement and the upgrading of the product(Maristella et. al.,2013).

Website evaluation is the use of research or investigative procedures to systematically determine the effectiveness of a web based information system on an ongoing basis. Evaluation plays a key role in organizational planning, monitoring website activities and services, and modifying goals and objectives on an ongoing basis. This is "formative" evaluation. In contrast, "summative" evaluation determines the degree to which the website is meeting set goals and user needs. Figure 2.7 illustrates this dual role. On the left side of the diagram, information discovered as part of the evaluation process feeds back into goal setting and planning. Ongoing evaluation is a vital source of information for agencies' planning processes. For example, an evaluation of current website user satisfaction may reveal usability issues with the current page design or information architecture. Planners may choose to change or modify goals based upon newly discovered problems or the achievement of previously set goals(Lawet. al., 2010).

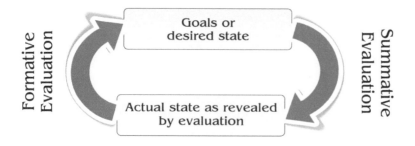

Fig. 2.7.Formative and Summative Evaluation.

Source:Mary Beth Rosson and John M. Carroll (Auth.),"Usability Engineering. Scenario-Based Development of Human-Computer Interaction" , 2001, p228.

On the right side of the diagram, evaluation determines the degree to which the organization has met stated goals. Developing goals and objectives with no follow-up effort to determine how well those objectives were actually accomplished significantly reduces the overall value of both planning and the use of assessment techniques(Mary & John, 2001). Based on the previous evaluation, if the organization had created a goal to improve site usability, they would then use evaluation to determine the degree to which the site's usability had improved. Both formative and summative evaluation efforts are important – although most organizations tend to concentrate on summative approaches. But for monitoring and ongoing improvement of services, formative evaluation (intended to improve, not prove) is essential (Thompson et. al., 2003; Dada, 2006).

Since the mid 1990s,interest in website evaluation has surged. One result has been the publication of a range of web "do-it-yourself" books that include advice on both design and evaluation. At the same time, researchers from the business, education and information science fields have sought to evaluate web sites based on many criteria including: web metrics, interface design, usability, comparison to peer organizations – benchmarking, fit with theoretical models of web site strategy, information quality, and hypertext structure.Web site evaluation has also become a popular topic within the trade press(Thompson et. al., 2003). A significant amount of web evaluation emphasis focuses on log analysis techniques and use of specific log analysis software such as Web-Trends and Web-tracker (Falahrastegar et. al., 2014).

There were suggested three criteria to apply in a case study approach in research: first, to be capable of researching the system in a natural setting; second, understand the complexity of the processes and interactions happening, and third, as a viable tool to research an area with little prior research. All of the data collected were qualitative. The author was a participant observer and directly involved in the design and development of the website through the usability company as usability professional. Participant observer is defined as "a researcher who participates in social activities with the subject of the study over an extended period of time" (Alsha & Saif, 2011; Baecker, 2014). Participant observation is a cornerstone of anthropology and less objectivity is sometimes an issue when researchers are directly involved in what is being researched. On the other hand, when the researchers are directly involved, they have access to a wealth of experience that is otherwise not accessible (Poltrock & Grudin, 1994; Cummings & Christopher, 2014). The roles of usability professional and researcher in this case was intertwined but data collected extended beyond that of the commercial work at hand; observations and follow-up interviews collected data discussing the attitudes throughout the work period. Assertions to the quality of the website and the work done was left to the team members of the project rather than the usability professional to decrease the issue of researcher objectivity. The data gathering was made up of actual documents produced and correspondence related to the project. These included emails, brainstorming sessions, meetings, conversations, and interviews at the end of the consultation period. This allowed for the interaction with individual team members working on the project and also helped in the understanding of complexity in relationships whilst working on a commercial design project. its gave opportunity to observe the reactions and attitudes of team members towards usability when implementing a structured framework, rather than just gathering information about what participants say about usability at various times throughout the consultation period (Williams & Beynon-Davies, 2004). There were a total of 20 people involved throughout the project with different groups involved at different times. The number of people involved does not include those who worked on the project but had no direct contact with the usability consultancy which included people working on coding and hardware required for the website. The case study was a unique opportunity that allowed the author to interact with two sections of the project. The first section did not start until the usability consultancy's involvement (the portal) and the other section was nearing the completion of the project; at least from a development perspective where much of the development had been done (the online services). This situation allowed the author to observe and record other team members' reactions and interactions with recommendations brought up by the usability analysis.

Working with two distinct sections of the project also allowed the author to implement Garrett's framework on one section (the portal) and try to do so on the other section (online services); and to compare and contrast the differences when a framework is implemented at the beginning and mid-project. (Garrett, 2002; Albert & Thomas, 2013). The framework was selected for use in this project because of the considered benefits to the real-world user not found in other frameworks, as discussed above. One of the most critical benefits is that it allowed communication between stakeholders without the use of overly technical terms through abstraction and with a concentration on end-user needs rather than what the developers can develop in the given amount of time or how much the budget can buy. The technical issues are then handled by the developers after the requirements from a usability perspective have been agreed upon by stakeholders. In the first meeting, the stakeholders were briefed on Garrett's framework and the stages of design were laid out.

Following detailed analysis of methods used for evaluation of web page usability, it can be found which of them apply certain solutions, have some qualities and which do not have. Based on review of reference books, own method of evaluation of webpage usability have been proposed in this respect. This method has some features of the other techniques but it is also distinguished by comprehensive evaluation. Table 2.5 presents the comparison of a proposed method and other methods, like: informal inspection method, guidelines review, consistency inspection, cognitive walkthrough, formal usability inspection.

- **Informal of inspection methods**

The main goal of heuristic evaluations is to identify any problems associated with the design of user interfaces. Usability consultant(Nielsen, 1994)developed this method on the basis of several years of experience in teaching and consulting aboutusability engineering (Balandet. al., 2010).

The simplicity of heuristic evaluation is beneficial at the early stages of design. This usability inspection method does not require user testing which can be burdensome due to the need for users, a place to test them and a payment for their time. Heuristic evaluation requires only one expert, reducing the complexity and expended time for evaluation. Most heuristic evaluations can be accomplished in a matter of days. The time required varies with the size of the artefact, its complexity, the purpose of the review, the nature of the usability issues that arise in the review, and the competence of the reviewers. Using heuristic evaluation prior to user testing will reduce the number and severity of design errors discovered by users. Although heuristic evaluation can uncover many major usability issues in a short period of time, a criticism that is often levelled is that results are highly influenced by the knowledge of the expert reviewer(s). This "one-sided" review repeatedly has different results than each type of testing un-covering a different set of problems (Nielsen, 1990).

- **Guidelines review**

The particular steps of application stage include design, coding, testing and release of application. The advantage of such a procedure is that the usability issues are resolved faster, so that greater number of usability problems can be found at one time. Disad-vantage is that it does not address the usability issue to efficiency.

- **Consistency inspection method:**

Consistency inspections ensure consistency across multiple products from the same development effort. For example, in a suite of office productivity applications, common functions should look and work the same whether the user is using the word processor, spreadsheet, presentation, or database program. Consistency inspections begin with a usability professional analyzing the interfaces to all of the products and noting the vari-ous ways that each product implements a particular user interaction or function. An evaluation team then meets, and using the usability analysis as a basis, negotiates and decides on the one golden implementation for the usability attributes of each product (Hom, 1998; Sivaji et. al.,2011).

- **Cognitive walkthrough**

The cognitive walkthrough method is a type of usability evaluation technique that fo-cuses on evaluating an (early) system design for learnability by exploration.The cogni-tive walkthrough helps an evaluator in examining the interplay between a user's inten-tions and the feedback provided by the system's interface. The cognitive walkthrough relies on a cognitive model of a novice user executing four steps in the context of a task the user is to perform: (1) the user would set a goal to be accomplished, (2) the user would inspect the available actions on the user screen (in the form of menu items, but-tons, etc.), (3) the user would select one of the available actions that seems to make progress toward his goal, and (4) the user would perform the action and evaluate the system's feedback for evidence that progress is being made toward his current goal(Jaspers, 2009).

The evaluator tries to answer on four questions: (1) will the user try to achieve the correct effect, (2) will the user notice that the correct action is available, (3) will the user associate the correct action with the desired effect, and, if the user performed the right action, (4) will the user notice that progress is being made toward accomplishment of his goal. If there are positive answers to all four questions, the execution of the specified action is found to be without usability flaws, if there is a negative answer to any of the four questions, the specified action is not free of usability problems(Jaspers, 2009). Cognitive walkthrough is largely applied to evaluate presentation aspects in the application interface. Its use is recommended in the advanced phases of the Web application development, for evaluating high fidelity prototypes for which the interaction functionalities already work. The typical cognitive walkthrough procedure prescribes that, on the basis of selected scenarios of use, a series of tasks are chosen to be performed on the interface by an expert evaluator.

Formal usability testing

It is a review of users' potential task performance with a product. It is completed by the product owner (i.e., the engineer who is designing the product) and a team of peers, looking for defects. A formal usability inspection has the following characteristics(Nielsen & Mack, 1994):

- A defect detection and description process: To detect defects, inspectors always use user profiles and step through task scenarios. While stepping these hypothetical users through tasks, inspectors apply a task performance model and heuristics. Then, inspectors describe these defects in a user-centered manner as suggested by the task performance model and heuristics.
- An inspection team: Inspectors represent various areas of knowledge, including, as appropriate: software, hardware, documentation, support, and human factors engineering. The method also defines the responsibilities that inspection team members have to the inspection process (i.e., a moderator, owner, inspectors, and a scribe).

- A structure within the usability lifecycle: Defect detection is framed within a structure of six logistical steps. These steps provide an effective and efficient process and link the inspection into the usability lifecycle.

Analysing Polish cities websites in the context of their usability, investigations made in 2013 by(Marcin & Joanna, 2013)should be mentioned. The study was based on multifaceted evaluation of the cities' websites in the context of their promotional role and communication functions. The evaluation comprised a questionnaire that aimed to answer whether the websites displayed a certain quality or not. Several different criteria were taken into account and they were divided into a few thematic areas: information about a municipality including address and telephone number, technical aspects, Web-site functionality and interactivity, media relations, communication with citizens and local community, communication with tourists, business information, and additional elements. The research was conducted in January 2013 and included all the capitals of Polish provinces. The evaluated websites were then placed in an overall ranking that presented their attractiveness, and their positions depended on the score that they achieved during the evaluation. In the research there were analysed eighteen websites of the following cities: *Białystok (www.bialystok.pl), Bydgoszcz (www.bydgoszcz.pl), Gdańsk (www.gdansk.pl), GorzówWlkp. (www.gorzow.pl), Katowice (www.katowice.eu), Kielce (www.um.kielce.pl), Kraków (www.krakow.pl), Lublin (www.lublin.eu), Łódź (www.uml.lodz.pl), Olsztyn (www.olsztyn.eu), Opole (www.opole.pl), Poznań (www.poznan.pl), Rzeszów (www.rzeszow.pl), Szczecin (www.szczecin.pl), Toruń (www.torun.pl), Warszawa (www.um.warszawa.pl), Wrocław (www.wroclaw.pl), Zielona Góra (www.zielona-gora.pl).*In order to conduct an effective evaluation of websites they were divided into groups described by letters.

Group A   was described as "Information about municipality with its address and telephone numbers",

Group B   was related to "Technical aspects of the Website", such as intuitive domain names (in Poland it means »name of the city.pl«),

Group C   referred to "Website functionality and interactivity". This thematic area consisted of fourteen important aspects such as: ask the president? The possibility of asking the city authority direct questions through a special form, "contact us" form; e-mail address to the city council with a domain name that corresponds with the city's domain, online office, print possibility, easy to navigate (for example through clear and easy menu and "home" button), site map, English version, other language version(s), search engine for the website content, up-to-date information.

Group D   referred to "Media relations" and content of this section was evaluated in three aspects: if there is any section addressed to the media, contact to a spokesman; are there news, press releases and photos available for the media.

Group E   was called "Communication with citizens and local community" and within this thematic area, information important for the citizens of the city was evaluated, for example social care and health, education and learning, jobs and careers, libraries, public transport, news, photo gallery, newsletter, FAQ, tools and forms for receiving feedback from website users (opinion surveys, chat rooms, guest book, have your say etc.).

Group F   described as "Communication with tourists" where all opinion relevant to tourists' and city visitors' point of view were evaluated. Among them there were: location of the city, tourist attractions, events calendar, accommodation information, additional interactive options (for example virtual tour in museums and other places), places to go, important information relevant to tourist (transport, services), and contact to tourist information. In addition, language versions and ease to find section for tourist was also scored.

Group G   "Investor Relations" was scored when there was a separate section for investors on the home page, at least two language versions of the website, information about tenders, investments in the city, strategic investors, investment incentives, contact for investors and business directory, additional relevant information, for example reasons for investing in the city, institutions supporting business development, recommendations for entrepreneurs.

Group H   was described as "additional elements" and included all extra options offered by the cities' websites, such as: website statistics, webcams in the city, virtual tour around the city.

The researcher assumed that if a city website displayed certain quality it was given one point for such quality, but if not, it was scored 0. If the evaluated quality was placed on the Public Information Bulletin (Avraham & Eran, 2008; Gębarowski, 2013).instead of the official city website, it did not score any points. When the evaluation was complete, points in every thematic area were summed up and the evaluated websites of the capitals of Polish provinces were placed in an overall ranking that presented their attractiveness, and their positions depended on the score that they achieved during the evaluation. The highest score that the website could gain was 73 points.

Following detailed analysis of methods used for evaluation of web page usability, it can be found that some of them apply certain solutions, have some parameters and the other don't. Based on review of reference books, the summary (Table 2.5) showing presence or absence of particular quality in the analysed methods was made.

Table 2.5. Summary of presence of particular qualities in methods of websites' evaluation

Website's evaluation methods / Parameters subject to analysis	Heuristic evaluation	Review and guidelines	Consistency inspection	Cognitive walkthrough	Formal usability testing
Webtracking system	–	–	–	–	–
Heuristic evaluation	+	–	+	+	+
Questionnaires	+	–	+	+	+
Number of answers to questions (Yes/No)	–	+	+	+	+
Syntactic distance measure	–	–	–	–	–
K-mean clustering	–	–	–	–	–
Likert scale	+	–	–	–	–
Page recognition system	–	–	–	–	–
Calculation of number of characters used in response on website	–	–	–	–	–
Calculation of average response time	+	+	–	–	–
Calculation of use of links	+	–	–	+	–

Website's evaluation methods / Parameters subject to analysis	Heuristic evaluation	Review and guide-lines	Consistency inspec-tion	Cognitive walkthrough	Formal usability test-ing
Calculation of response quality	+	+	+	−	+
User's evaluation FUF (Flexibility, User-satisfaction , and few errors)	+	−	+	−	+
Web building according to evaluation results	−	−	+	−	−
Data evaluation and validation	−	+	−	−	−
Use of criteria for website evaluation	+	+	+	+	+
Quantitative data analysis	+	+	−	−	−
Qualitative data analysis	+	+	+	+	+
Consistency of terminology	−	−	+	−	−
Formal meeting and discussion	−	+	−	−	+
Creation of a team subject to test	−	+	+	+	+

Source: own elaboration

(+) means absence of a parameter (not present);

(-) means presence of a parameter.

Table 2.5.Shows that specified qualities are not always used in the analysed methods for websites' evaluation. Thus, the author of this dissertation will fill the identified gap by developing a method, which includes majority of those parameters and therefore will provide more accuracy in websites evaluation.

3. LOCAL GOVERNMENT WEBSITE ANALYSIS AND EVAL-
UATION METHOD DEVELOPED BY THE RESEARCHER

3.1 pre-selection of internet services in the local governments units

The first step is selection of LGU websites subject to research procedure, including evaluation of their usability in the webtracking system developed by the author of
this thesis.

Popularity analysis of LGU websites

Websites of the biggest Polish cities have been chosen to perform analysis due to
their potential attractiveness to foreign users. This attractiveness refers to touristic values of a region, potential in respect of opportunity to conduct business activities by foreign investors and offered business opportunities to cooperate with local partners.

As the result of this analysis carried out based on LGU websites of bigger Polish
cities there were selected 20 websites, which according to alexa.com and ipsong.com
had the most visitors, both Polish and (Table 3.1). Data refers to the year 2012. Information on searching a place, website creation date, latest update, hosting name, number
of visits etc. were collected as well.

Table 3.1. Selected information about websites of Polish cities (2012)

City	Website	Website date creation	Expired	Last update	Polish visitors (%)	German visitors (%)	American visitors (%)	British visitors (%)	French visitors (%)
Poznań	www.poznan.pl	1995.01.01	2012.12.31	2007.09.03	89	3.20	0.70	n/a	0.00
Szczecin	szczecin.pl	2003.03.25	Not defined	2006.02.09	87.70	5.80	1.60	0.80	0.00
Warszawa	warszawa.pl	2003.03.25	Not defined	2006.02.09	93	n/a	0.70	n/a	0.60
Kraków	www.krakow.pl	2001.01.01	2012.12.31	2005.01.05	90.80	1.40	0.70	1	0.80
Wrocław	www.wroclaw.pl	2003.03.25	Not defined	2006.02.09	93.60	0.60	n/a	n/a	n/a
Gdańsk	gdansk.pl	2003.06.09	2012.06.08	2011.02.03	83.50	4.10	n/a	4.90	n/a
Łódź	www.lodz.pl	n/a	Not defined	n/a	88.00	n/a	n/a	n/a	n/a

City	Website	Website date creation	Expired	Last update	Polish visitors (%)	German visitors (%)	American visitors (%)	British visitors (%)	French visitors (%)
Bydgoszcz	bydgoszcz.pl	2003.03.25	Not defined	2006.02.09	93.10	1.20	0.80	n/a	n/a
Lublin	lublin.pl	1995.01.01	2012.07.29	2011.07.01	91.60	1.60	0.80	n/a	n/a
Katowice	katowice.pl	2003.03.25	Not defined	2006.02.09	94.1	0.8	n/a	0.9	n/a
Bialystok	www.bialystok.pl	2003.03.25	not defined	2006.02.09	93.90	n/a	n/a	1.20	n/a
Gdynia	gdynia.pl	1995.01.01	2012.12.31	2011.02.03	92.30	n/a	n/a	n/a	n/a
Częstochowa	czestochowa.pl	2003.04.01	2012.03.31	2005.04.05	96.90	n/a	n/a	n/a	n/a
Sosnowiec	www.sosnowiec.pl	2003.03.25	Not defined	2006.02.09	88.70	n/a	n/a	n/a	n/a
Radom	www.radom.pl/page	2003.03.25	Not defined	2006.02.09	93.80	n/a	1.70	n/a	n/a
Kielce	www.kielce.eu	1995.01.01	2012.12.31	1995.01.01	92.80	2.30	n/a	n/a	n/a
Gliwice	gliwice.pl	1995.01.01	2012.12.31	2003.09.16	89.8	n/a	n/a	6.0	n/a
Toruń	www.torun.pl	1995.01.01	2012.12.31	1995.01.01	89.50	2.90	n/a	n/a	n/a
Bytom	www.bytom.pl/pl	2003.03.25	Not defined	2006.02.09	93.30	n/a	n/a	n/a	n/a
Zabrze	www.um.zabrze.pl	1995.01.01	2012.03.08	2011.08.10	77.40	n/a	n/a	n/a	n/a

Source: own elaboration

Charts 1 and 2 shows the percentage of Polish and foreign users, accordingly, visiting LGU websites.

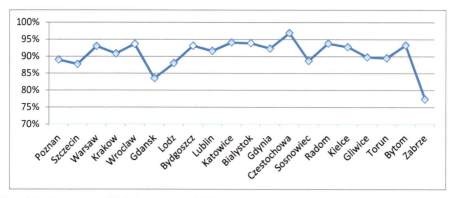

Chart 3.1. Percentage of Polish visitors in 2012

Source: own elaboration

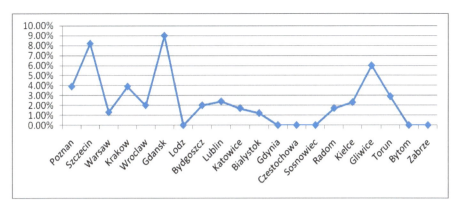

Chart 3.2. Percentage of foreign visitors in 2012
Source: own elaboration

According to Chart 1 **Polish visitors** represented the highest number in Czestochowa website's visits, while **Zabrze** website had the lowest proportion. Chart 2 shows that **Gdansk** had higher percentage of foreign visitors, while **Gdynia, Czestochowa, Sosnowiec, Bytom**and **Zabrze** had the lowest number of visitors or no foreign visitors over 2012 at all. Four cities have been excluded from examination, because they did not provide information in English on their websites. These cities were **Wroclaw, Sosnowiec, Toruń**and**Zabrze**.Websites progress curvesfor all cities during period 2012-2015 can shows in *appendix A,B.*

Analysis of mechanisms and communication procedures on 20 LGU websites.

This stage of research was related to testing communication capability and interactivity of LGU websites by measuring response time to queries posted to contact e–mail of these websites. E-mails were sent to each city's webmaster, inquiring about business investment and tourism. The response time was recorded accordingly. Cities with a shorter response time were evaluated to have the best management and communication capability.

Table 3.2 presents results of measurement of each city's response time and interactivity with foreign users. Only **five** cities responded to inquiries, some cities do not have a recorded response time. The shorter response times was recorded for **Radom** and **Lublin**. The longest response time was recorded for **Bydgoszcz** (three days). Other cities gave no response.

Table 3.2. Response time measurement for each of 20 selected Cities

Item	City	e-mail	Time of a post	Response time	Date of posting an inquiry	Response date
1	Poznań	promocja@um.poznan.pl	21:05		9/1/2012	n/a
2	Szczecin	Webmaster	21:06		9/1/2012	n/a
3	Warszawa	Webmaster	21:15		9/1/2012	n/a
4	Kraków	Webmaster	21:19	-	9/1/2012	n/a
5	Wrocław	araw@araw.pl	21:23		9/1/2012	n/a
6	Gdańsk	umg@gdansk.gda.pl	21:41		9/1/2012	n/a
7	Łódź	uml@uml.lodz.pl	21:45		9/1/2012	n/a
8	Bydgoszcz	urzad@um.bydgoszcz.pl	21:59	12:10	9/1/2012	12/1/2012
9	Lublin	inwestorzy@lublin.eu	22:10	15:20	10/1/2012	11/1/2012
10	Katowice	webmaster@um.katowice.pl	22:14		10/1/2012	n/a
11	Białystok	redakcja@um.bialystok.pl	22:19		10/1/2012	n/a
12	Gdynia	polityka-nieruchomosci@gdynia.pl	22:27	12:05	10/1/2012	12/01/2012
13	Częstochowa	webmaster@czestochowa.pl	22:47		10/1/2012	n/a
14	Sosnowiec	cim@um.sosnowiec.pl	22:51		10/1/2012	n/a
15	Radom	e-mail Box Sender	22:57	11:52	10/1/2012	11/1/2012
16	Kielce	webmaster@um.kielce.pl	23:20		10/1/2012	n/a
17	Gliwice	boi@um.gliwice.pl	23:27	12:05	10/1/2012	12/1/2012
18	Toruń	boi@um.torun.pl	18:39		11/1/2012	n/a
19	Bytom	um@um.bytom.pl sp@um.bytom.pl	19:11		11/1/2012	n/a
20	Zabrze	rkobos@gis.um.zabrze.pl	19:18		11/1/2012	n/a

Source: own elaboration

According to the results in Table 3.3, the majority of cities did not have the best services in websites. This is because there are no developed mechanisms or no people responsible for contact and answers through electronic communication services. It may also result from underestimation of such a form of communication or skills to communicate in English.

3.2 Use of VMCM method to select representative websites

Selection of 8 websites of LGU for further detailed analysis.

Selected on the previous stage LGU websites (20 cities) were subject to detailed analysis with respect to find certain information. Both Polish and English versions of websites were examined. Factors subject to analysis are presented in Table 3.3.

Table 3.3. Main factors and sub- factors applied for Polish Local Government Websites analysis

Main factors	Sub-factors							
Education	Kindergartens	Primary school	Secondary school	High school	University and higher education	Books, libraries		
Tourism	Mountains area	Rivers and sea area	Forests	Archaeological and antiques area	Recreational area	Museums		
Hotels	Hotel 4-5 star	Hotel 1-3 star	Hostels and guesthouses	Motels	Youth hostels			
Restaurants	Pubs and clubs	Bars	Cafe	Dining facilities	Canteens	Restaurants		
Transportation	Airports	Parking	Buses	Taxi	Trams	Trains	Timetables	Ticket prices
Booking	Dormitory	Apartments	Rooms	Other				
Investments	Investment offer	Investment services	Locations	Information about investment	Investment incentives	IT	News and publications	
Health	Medical call centre	Pharmacies	Emergency aid	Dentists	English speaking GP	Emergency services		
Business	Chamber of Commerce	Business centres	Economic zones	Offers provided by cities	Conferences	Companies	Information	

Source: own elaboration

To evaluate each of 20 LGU website a set of 10 quality criteria, presented in Table 3.4. Was applied.

Table 3.4.Website Quality Evaluation Criteria.

No	Criterion	Definition
1	Navigability	This criterion measures how easy one can browse the site, facility to return to the homepage and how easy one can find relevant information, how many links are required to reach another place on the site and what searching tools does the site provide. (Smith, 2001; González, 2004).
2	Speed	This criterion refers to speed of getting response, facility to access to links (Bilsel et. al., 2006), and website loading time (Smith, 2001).
3	Links	Is refers to links to websites of another local and state government organizations (Büyüközkan& Ruan, 2007), various national parks, organizations for natural environment protection, tourism organisations and travel agencies and other related websites.
4	Relevancy	This criterion includes relevant depth, scope, and completeness of information (Younghwa et. al.,2006).Different parts of the website should be designed to meet the needs of different group of visitors (Mei et. al., 2005), such as travelers, researchers, students, and local citizens.
5	Richness	This criterion refers to detailed level and scope of information content. That is, whether information displayed on the website is rich in content (Bilselet. al., 2006).
6	Currency	This criterion refers to provision of up-to-date information. Last update dates are a critical way of notifying users of the currency of content (Younghwa et. al. 2006; Smith, 2001).
7	Attractiveness	This criterion refers to general website attractiveness, method of content presentation, through such elements like graphics, online games, screensavers, opportunity to download files, etc. (Cao et. al., 2005; Huizingh, 2000; González, 2004).
8	Security	This criterion refers to matters related to trust and security of the website (Ho & Lee, 2007). Security mechanisms for its users' personal and private data protection should be applied, as well as measures to prevent the content from being damaged (Bueyuekoezkan& Ruan, 2007; Chu, 2001).
9	Personalization	This criterion involves possibility to customize websites according to users' preferences (Lee & Kozar, 2006). Proper customization of the website content is one of the vital aspects of website browsing (Ho& Lee, 2007).
10	Responsiveness	This criterion deals with the provision of information on FAQs and prompt assistance in solving problems (Ahn et. al., 2007; Ho&Lee, 2007). Different management systems should be made available (Lee &Kozar, 2006),

Source: own elaboration

Assessment was carried out using a Likert scale in a range from 0-9. Every factor was subject to evaluation.

To build aggregate measure using VMCM, the procedure presented in Fig. 3.1. was applied. This measure was used to range analysed websites.

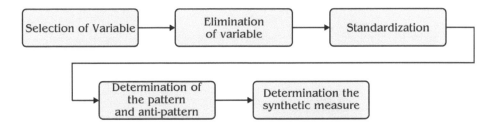

Fig. 3.1.Procedure of building the aggregate measure.

Source:Nermendet. al., Application of web-tracking methods to research local–government websites' utility, P. 224.

Procedure of building the aggregate measure using VMCM method consists of five stages: setting the evaluation criteria, elimination of criteria of small variability, normalization, construction of pattern and anti-pattern and calculation the value of measure, ranging.

- **Selection of Variables**

In terms of selection of variables, it is possible to apply statistical and formal methods of selection, and/or the analyst can select the variables according to the existing economic theory or knowledge about researched issues, where his experience plays an important role. Regardless of the preferred approach, the selection of variables is done in such a manner so as to reproduce, describe and measure the investigated phenomenon most accurately. The variables are put in the observation matrix (Nermend, 2009):

$$X = \begin{bmatrix} x_{1_1} & x_{2_1} & \cdots & x_{k_1} & \cdots & x_{M_1} \\ x_{1_2} & x_{2_2} & \cdots & x_{k_2} & \cdots & x_{M_2} \\ \cdots & \cdots & \cdots & \cdots & \cdots & \cdots \\ x_{1_i} & x_{2_i} & \cdots & x_{k_i} & \cdots & x_{M_i} \\ \cdots & \cdots & \cdots & \cdots & \cdots & \cdots \\ x_{1_N} & x_{2_N} & \cdots & x_{k_N} & \cdots & x_{M_N} \end{bmatrix} \quad (3.1)$$

where N is the number of objects, M is the number of variables, and x_{i_j} is the value of the i th variable for the j th object.

- **Elimination of Variables**

In the existing literature, the elimination of variables is usually performed by using the coefficient of significance(Kukuła, 2000):

$$V_{x_i} = \frac{\sigma_i}{\bar{x}_i},$$ (3.2)

where x_i is the i th variable, σ_i is the standard deviation of the i th variable, and $\bar{x}_i$ is the mean value of the i th variable, and where:

$$\bar{x}_i = \frac{\sum_{j=1}^{N} x_{i_j}}{N},$$ (3.3)

and:

$$\sigma_i = \sqrt{\frac{\sum_{j=1}^{N} \left(x_{i_j} - \bar{x}_i\right)^2}{N-1}}.$$ (3.4)

The variables whose significance factors values are within the <-1,0,1> range, constitute quasi-constant variables. Such variables should be eliminated from the set of variables under consideration.

- **Standardization**

Variables used in the studies are heterogeneous, in fact they describe different properties of the objects. Various units may be used in measuring different properties, which further hinder any arithmetic operations to be used by individual procedures. For this reason, the next step to be performed in the construction of the aggregate measure is to *standardize the variables*. This process not only leads to the elimination of units of measurement, but also to the equalization of variable values. Standardization is one of the most commonly used methods of normalization (Nermend, 2009):

$$x'_i = \frac{A_i}{\sigma_i} \quad , \qquad\qquad\qquad\qquad (3.5)$$

where the A_i factor can be defined arbitrarily, for example:

$$A_i = x_i - \bar{x}_i \quad , \qquad\qquad\qquad\qquad (3.6)$$

given that x'_i is the normalized value of the i-th variable for the j-th object.

- **Determination of the Pattern and Anti-Pattern**

After normalizing the variables, the next step is the determination of pattern and anti–pattern of investigated phenomenon. Collected variables are divided into stimulants and destimulants(Hellwig, 1968). The criterion of division is the impact of each of the selected variables on the level of development of the investigated phenomenon (unit). Variables that have a positive, stimulating effect on the level of unit are called stimulants, as opposed to inhibitory variables, called destimulants. Sometimes the optimal level of development for a given variable is achieved, which is then called the nominate. In Hellwig's measure, a pattern is defined on the basis of the values of variables. The coordinates of the pattern in Hellwig's measure are defined as the maximum value of stimulants and minimum value of destimulants. The nominates are usually transformed into stimulants or destimulants. In vector measures, it is not the position of the pattern that is important, but rather the direction (vector) indicating the position of the best object. The direction is determined on the basis of the pattern that is characterized by high values of both stimulants and destimulants. The anti–pattern and pattern can be taken as real objects. On the basis of first and third quartile (Kolenda, 2006), it is also possible to automatically determine both the pattern and the anti–pattern. At the same time, variables for stimulants in the third quartile and variables for destimulants in the first quartile are considered to be the coordinates of the pattern:

$$x'_{i\,w} = \begin{cases} x'_{i\,k_{\mathrm{III}}} & \text{for stimulants} \\ x'_{i\,k_{\mathrm{I}}} & \text{for destimulan ts} \end{cases} \qquad\qquad (3.7)$$

where:

$x'_i{}_w$ is the value of the ith normalized variable for the pattern, $x'_i{}_{k_I}$ is the value of the ith normalized variable for the first quartile, and $x'_i{}_{k_m}$ is the value of the ith normalized variable for the third quartile.

In the case of anti–pattern, the procedure is reversed. To be more exact, the values of the stimulants from the first quartile and the values of destimulants from the third quartile constitute the coordinates of the pattern:

$$x'_i{}_{aw} = \begin{cases} x'_i{}_{k_I} & \text{for stimulants} \\ x'_i{}_{k_m} & \text{for destimulan ts} \end{cases} \qquad (3.8)$$

where $x'_i{}_{aw}$ is the value of the i-th normalized variable for the anti-pattern.

- **Quartile**

Quartiles are measurements of location for a distribution of observations. Quartiles separate a distribution into four parts. There are three quartiles is given distribution. In each quartile, 25% of the total observations can be found. The first and third quartiles constitute values of the 25th and 75th percentiles, respectively. In a set of numbers, a percentile is the value below which a certain percentage of the numbers in the set can be found (Dodge, 2008). The first and third quartiles are presented in Figure 3.2.

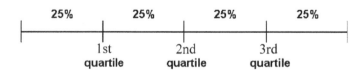

Fig 3.2.Determining the 1st and 3rd quartile.

Source: Dodge, Y. (2008).The concise encyclopedia of statistics.Springer Science & Business Media.

Note that the second quartile equals the **median**.

$$P_p(x) = N\frac{x}{100}, \qquad \text{for integer } N\frac{x}{100} \qquad\qquad (3.9)$$

$$\text{for fractional } N\frac{x}{100}$$

When we have observations grouped into classes, quartiles are determined as follows:

1. Determine the class where the quartile is found:

   - **First quartile**: class for which the relative cumulative frequency exceeds 25%.

   - **Second quartile**: class for which the relative cumulative frequency exceeds 50%.

   - **Third quartile**: class for which the relative cumulative frequency exceeds 75%.

2. Calculate the value of the quartile depending on the assumption according to which the observations are uniformly distributed in each class. The jth quartile $Qj$is:

$$Q_j = L_j + \left[\frac{n\cdot\frac{j}{4} - \sum f\,inf}{f\,j}\right]\cdot C_j. \qquad\qquad (3.10)$$

where$L_j$is the lower limit of the class of quartile Q_j, n is the total number of observations,f_{inf} is the sum of frequencies lower than the class of the quartile, $f_j$is the frequency of the class of quartile Qj, and $c_j$is the size of the **interval** of the class of quartile Q_j.

The patterns specified in this way are insensitive to the values of variables in atypical objects. As opposed to the measure proposed by Hellwig, they are not the ideal objects to which other items should drift. They only provide direction in which all the objects should evolve. Another way of determining this direction could also be to adopt a real object as both pattern and anti–pattern. Significantly, those do not need to be the best and the worst objects – they should simply be characterized by suitable proportions of the variables.

– **Determination of the Synthetic Measure.**

In the vector space, the values of the variables in the examined objects are interpreted as coordinates of the vectors. Each object represents a specific direction in space. The difference in pattern and anti-pattern is also a vector designating the direction in space. Along this direction, the value of synthetic measure is calculated for each object, providing the one dimensional coordinate system. Given that, the process of determining the measure becomes the process of determining the coordinate in this coordinates system, which can be illustrated by the following formula (Nermend, 2006), (Nermend , 2009):

$$
m_{s\eta \atop j} = \frac{\sum\limits_{i=1}^{M}\left(x'_i - x'_{i \atop aw} \right)\left(x'_i - x'_{i \atop aw} \right)}{\sum\limits_{i=1}^{M}\left(x'_{i \atop w} - x'_{i \atop aw} \right)^2}
\tag{3.11}
$$

For the measure constructed in this way, all objects that are better than the anti–pattern and worse than the pattern will be characterized by the value of measure ranging from zero to one. Hence, the pattern will have the value of measure equal to one, while the anti–pattern equals zero. It is feasible to determine the values of measure in objects that are better than the pattern because they will have a value of measure greater than one. Objects that are worse than the anti–pattern will have a negative measure. Thus, one can easily determine the object's position in the ranking, in reference to the pattern and the anti–pattern.

– **Method of Grouping**

For each city's website,studyassign aggregate measure, calculated as presented above. The cities are divided into predefined number of groups (clusters), based on some heuristics. For clustering, study used the K–means clustering, a partitioning method that partitions data into k mutually exclusive clusters (groups)and returns the index of the cluster to which it has assigned each observation (data).

K - means clustering treats each observation as an object having a location in space. It finds a clustering partition in which objects in a cluster are as close to each other as possible, and as far from objects in other clusters as possible. Each cluster in the partition is defined by its member objects and by its centroid, or center. The centroid for each cluster is the point to which the sum of squared distances from all objects in that cluster is minimized.

K–means uses an iterative algorithm that minimizes the sum of distances from each object to its cluster centroid, over all clusters. This algorithm moves objects between clusters until the sum cannot be decreased further. The result is a set of clusters that are as compact and well - separated as possible.

Based on received results of aggregate measure websites were ranged and grouped into 4 classes by K-means methods (following the procedure available in reference books).Aggregate measures were constructed for the year 2013, for Polish and English versions of websites (the data resources can be found in *appendix D* for Polish version and *Appendix E* for English version).

Results of selection of city websites are presented in Table 3.5 (for Polish versions) and Table 3.6 (for English versions).

Table 3.5.Selection of eight representative websites on the basis of K-means method (year 2013, Polish version).

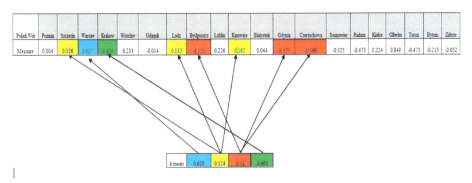

Source: author's own work

Websites of the following cities were selected: Szczecin, Warszawa, Kraków, Łódź, Bydgoszcz, Katowice, Gdynia and Częstochowa.

Tab. 3.6.Selection of eight representative websites on the basis of K-means method (year 2013, English version).

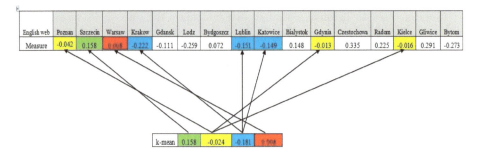

English web	Poznan	Szczecin	Warsaw	Krakow	Gdansk	Lodz	Bydgoszcz	Lublin	Katowice	Bialystok	Gdynia	Czestochowa	Radom	Kielce	Gliwice	Bytom
Measure	-0.042	0.158	0.008	-0.222	-0.111	-0.259	0.072	-0.151	-0.149	0.148	-0.013	0.335	0.225	-0.016	0.291	-0.273

k-mean	0.158	-0.024	-0.181	0.008

Source: author's own work

Tab. 3.6 shows four clusters. First cluster includes one city (Poznań), the second cluster includes three cities (Szczecin, Gdynia and Kielce); the third cluster includes three cities (Kraków, Katowice and Lublin); Fourth class includes one city (Warszawa).

3.3 Selection of information categories for LGU (questionnaire)

The next stage referred to analysis of type of information that could be desired by LGU websites users involved in business, investments and tourism. This information would allow including desired features at design or optimization phase of LGU website creation.

To carry out analysis a questionnaire including questions grouped into three information categories: investments, business and tourism were employed. For each category 33 questions have been formulated and consulted with **Prof. drhab.DariuszZarzecki,** expert in strategy in investment at the faculty of management. Consultations concerned types and pattern for questions included in the questionnaire form. The questionnaire was sent to representatives of business and students coming from different countries: **Malaysia, China, Dubai, Iraq, Saudi Arabia, Oman, the US, Sweden, Ukraine, and Poland.** The role of users was to provide answers on 11 questions according to specialization (11 questions for each category of information). Each question was evaluated on a Likert scale with five scores. The questions were assessed as very good, good, average, poor, and very poor, which were converted into numbers 100, 75, 50, 25, 0, respectively according to z (Tsai et. al.,2010). The quality and importance of the questions assigned to each category were recorded. As a result, five questions were selected, assessed as very important or important for each considered category (investment, tourism and business). In total, there were 15 questions concerning the evaluation of the three mentioned categories.

As previous research in local government websites found, the effectiveness of e–government online services helps determine to what extent citizens are satisfied (Guo & Lu, 2004; Huang, 2005). The questionnaires can be used to determine points of view regarding ideas, activities, previous experiences and future plans. They can collect straightforward data on a large number of people for exploration of the research sample (Creswell, 2013; Lowe, 2003).Thus, a questionnaire survey was selected as a research technique to explore the preferences of citizens, in order to assess the quality of information in local government websites. Questionnaires also reveal to what extent the government provides required information and citizens' preferences.

Thirty - three people completed a survey by questionnaire. The results of question selection are presented in Tab. 3.7. This table includes 5 questions for each information category. These questions have been implemented into the developed web-tracking system.

Table 3.7.Questions Nominated and Used in the Web-tracking System (Simplified Model).

No	Category	Question
1	Investment	Did you find investment offers on this city's website?
2	Investment	Did you find investor services on this city's website?
3	Investment	Did you find information about potential locations of investment on this website?
4	Investment	Did you find any contact information for an office to help you to receive more information about city investments on this city's website?
5	Investment	Did you find any incentives for investment on this city's website?
1	Business	Did you find information about a chamber of commerce on this website?
2	Business	Did you find information about special economic zones on this city's website?
3	Business	Did you find any ideas about business experiences previously in this city?
4	Business	Did you find any firms or companies working in this city mentioned on this website?

No	Category	Question
5	Business	Did you find information about business service centers on this city's website?
1	Tourism	Did you find any information about tourist or travel agencies on this city's website?
2	Tourism	Did you find any tourist information points on this city's website?
3	Tourism	Did you find any tourist services listed on this city's website? For example, hotel booking, museum ticket, boat booking, zoo ticket booking, etc.
4	Tourism	Did you find any offers for hotels or accommodations on this city's website?
5	Tourism	Did you find any tourist maps on this city's website?

Source: own elaboration.

System stores information for all the users, cities and inquires to facilitate calculation and analysis in Matlab environment, what was executed in the following research stage. In addition system records response time, number and type of links, website identification, number of characters, quality of information on the website and quality of response.*Appendix G* can shows the initial questionnairemodel.

3.4. Architecture of the webtracking system

The research procedure (detailed in Fig. 1) assumed creating a model of a webtracking system which purpose was to obtain information about cities' website by means of users' behavior as they browse LGU websites. The system has an embedded explorer, allowing the users to browse and navigate the system. The web-tracking system was built in V.B.Net language.

The web-tracking system records and tracks all operations performed as the user browses and searches in the embedded explorer in a system. Three main information categories have been examined in the system: investment, business, and tourism. The system cooperates with a knowledge base to recognize the type of webpage being viewed before the user answers each question. Database contains key words for mentioned categories. The system compares the words on a given webpage with the database to assign a webpage to one of the three main types. Figure 3.3 shows the home page of the proposed web-tracking (electronic questionnaire) system.

Fig. 3.3. The home page of web-tracking (electronic questionnaire) system
Source: own elaboration

System architecture includes two databases: input data and output data. Input database includes 15 questions, eight links to city websites and knowledge base. Output data include seven data categories:

- answers for questions (yes/no),
- users' evaluations of quality of information on www (0-9),
- number of links followed and sequence of link's selection (user trace),
- recorded time required to answer a question,
- number of characters identifying each page,
- webpage category (investment, business, tourism),
- rank of FUF (Flexibility, User-satisfaction and Few errors) , rated 0-9.

In the test participants/users are asked to give their hedonic opinion to a questions sample by choosing and marking one of nine alternatives, (ranging from 1 = like extremely to 9 = dislike extremely). The 9-point hedonic scale is nowadays present in several different appearances (Svensson, 2012).

Usability testing involves eight city web pages. Data analysis is performed separately for each question. Architecture of web-tracking system is presented in Fig 3.4.

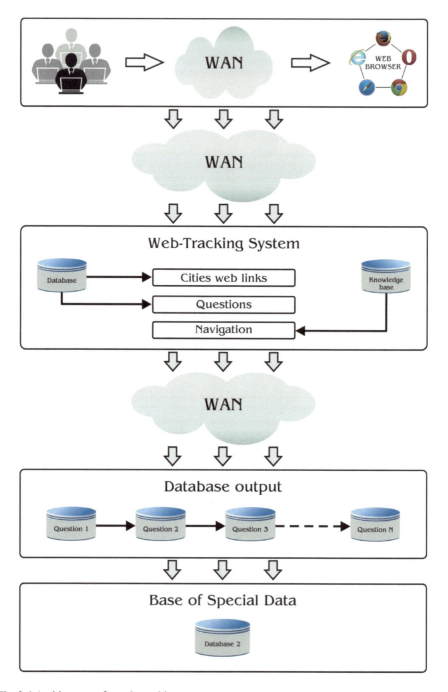

Fig. 3.4.Architecture of a web-tracking system

Source: own elaboration

Figure 3.5 shows main elements of the web-tracking system relating to data collection from users and recording of results in a database. Flowchart of testing process of the web-tracking system is presented in Fig 3.5.

Shipping Process Flowchart

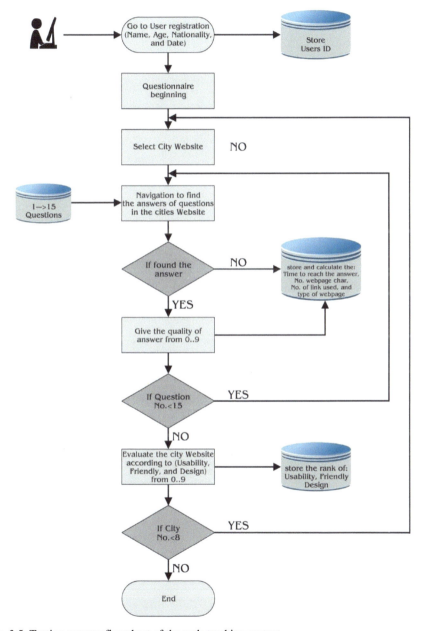

Fig. 3.5. Testing process flowchart of the web-tracking system

Source: own elaboration

Flowchart (Fig 3.6) illustrates all stages of websites testing in web-tracking system, which starts following user's registration. Basic personal data like user's name, age, nationality are recorded in the database.

Fig. 3.6. User's registration page in the webtracking system

Source: own elaboration

When the user answers all 15 questions, then he or she evaluates the city website's FUF (scores 0 to 9). Next, the user selects another city to examine and follows the same procedure for each city. This data is collected in the database of the web-tracking system. All registration data can be found in *appendix C.*

4. REFERENCE MODEL FOR LGU WEBSITE

4.1. Choice of indicators for the reference model and usability analysis of LGU websites

The next step of research procedure was survey conducted on 119 users from different countries (***Iraq, China, Ukraine, Poland***) with web-tracking system. The goal of the research was to find required information on eight previously selected LGU websites. The scope of this information was in accordance with what was received in the previous step of research (three thematic groups, each including 5 issues). For example information was sought on business opportunities for investors, access to tourist information or information regarding special economic zones. Subject to analysis was time required to find an answer to submitted question, number of clicks to reach the desired webpage, number of users who reached required information as well as usability of webpage, user's satisfaction, number of mistakes made during searching for information (scores 0-9). The examples of output data obtained from the electronic questionnaire, using web-tracking system are presented in Table 4.1.

Table 4.1. The examples of output data obtained from the electronic questionnaire from one user (UID – user ID, City ID miasta, QNo – question number, Qans – answer to question (yes/no), Qlty –information quality of answer (0-9), QClass – type of webpage,nolinks - number of links, Qtime - response time).

UID	City ID	Qno	Qans	Qlty	Qtime	Qlink	QClass	Nc	no links
8	3	2	No	0	5	www.um.warszawa.pl/en	investments	40482	3
8	3	3	Yes	3	11	www.um.warszawa.pl/en	investments	40482	3
8	3	4	Yes	4	22	www.um.warszawa.pl/en	investments	25329	3
8	3	5	Yes	6	10	www.um.warszawa.pl/en	investments	25329	4
8	3	12	No	0	7	www.um.warszawa.pl/en	investments	25329	4
8	3	13	Yes	5	18	www.um.warszawa.pl/en	investments	30759	3
8	3	14	No	0	4	www.um.warszawa.pl/en	investments	30759	2
8	3	15	Yes	7	9	www.um.warszawa.pl/en	investments	30759	2
8	3	16	Yes	7	7	www.um.warszawa.pl/en	investments	30759	2
8	3	32	Yes	7	29	www.um.warszawa.pl/en	investments	40896	4
8	3	34	Yes	5	29	www.warsawtour.pl/en	investments	22018	1
8	3	35	Yes	3	8	www.warsawtour.pl/en	investments	22018	3
8	3	37	Yes	9	26	www.warsawtour.pl/en/	investments	23229	2

UID	City ID	Qno	Qans	Qlty	Qtime	Qlink	QClass	Nc	no links
8	3	38	Yes	7	6	www.warsawtour.pl/en/	investments	23229	3
8	4	1	No	0	54	www.krakow.pl/biznes	investments	42697	1
8	4	2	No	0	8	www.krakow.pl/biznes	investments	42697	3
8	4	3	Yes	3	20	www.krakow.pl/biznes	investments	42697	4
8	4	4	Yes	5	7	www.krakow.pl/biznes	investments	42697	3
8	4	5	Yes	5	10	www.krakow.pl/biznes	investments	42697	4
8	4	12	No	0	4	www.krakow.pl/biznes	investments	42697	4
8	4	13	No	0	7	www.krakow.pl/biznes	investments	42697	3
8	4	14	No	0	5	www.krakow.pl/biznes	investments	42697	3
8	4	15	No	0	11	www.krakow.pl/biznes	investments	42697	2
8	4	16	Yes	7	6	www.krakow.pl/biznes	investments	42697	1
8	4	32	Yes	7	7	www.krakow.pl/biznes	investments	42697	1
8	4	34	Yes	7	12	www.krakow.pl/biznes	investments	42697	5
8	4	35	Yes	9	4	www.krakow.pl/biznes	investments	42697	5
8	4	37	Yes	9	6	www.krakow.pl/biznes	investments	42697	3
8	4	38	Yes	9	6	www.krakow.pl/biznes	investments	42697	3

Source: Own elaboration.

In addition, data related the user's assessment of FUF (Flexibility, User-satisfaction, Few errors) were obtained from web-tracking system and this referred to every city. After giving answers related to a given city, the user rated a website with 0-9 scale, Table 4.2 shows a simplified model for the user's assessment of FUF.

Table 4.2.Part of a simplified model for the user's assessment of FUF (foreign users).

User ID	City ID	Flexibility (F)	User's satisfaction (U)	Few errors (F)
23	1	6	7	3
23	2	6	6	2
23	3	8	7	3
23	10	9	9	2
23	6	7	6	3
23	12	6	5	4
23	4	6	5	3
23	16	6	6	3

Source: Ownelaboration.

Table 4.2 shows the simplified model for assessment provided by one user, who finished evaluation of all cities according to FUF factors. Analogous data were obtained for two language versions of each website. All data can be found in *appendix F*.

Following the users' testing, data collected by web-tracking system were subject to detailed analysis. As the result time required to get the answer, number of clicks to reach desired web page, number of users who reached required information as well as usability, user's satisfaction, number of mistakes during searching for information etc. were determined.

Average time to find the answer to the question

Average time to answer a question was computed by separate calculations for every city and question. Data file was loaded to Matlab and data entered to the matrix. They were ordered there in the sequence from the shortest to the longest time required to answer every question. Then average time was calculated. Table 4.3 indicates the average time required by foreign users, while Table 4.4 shows average time required by Polish users. These tables include data related to every question (1-15) and all LGU websites in question.

Presented data shows that average time required by foreign user was longer than by domestic ones because there is more information provided in Polish than in English. A1 group contains information regarding investments, A2 business, A3 tourism.

Table 4.3. Matrix A presents average time required by foreign users.

City	\(A_1\) Investments					\(A_2\) Business					\(A_3\) Tourism				
	Q1	Q2	Q3	Q4	Q5	Q6	Q7	Q8	Q9	Q10	Q11	Q12	Q13	Q14	Q15
Poznań	73.3	48.2	42.8	48.4	36.4	60.4	41.4	22.9	48.4	28.0	46.4	19.8	31.2	25.0	20.5
Szczecin	49.9	38.5	37.0	51.1	37.2	34.7	21.2	17.9	35.5	24.5	47.8	17.4	24.0	24.7	24.3
Warszawa	42.3	34.9	29.7	36.7	20.4	46.5	29.3	15.2	42.0	14.8	38.4	18.4	21.4	16.9	13.5
Kraków	85.9	16.4	12.4	16.1	15.9	23.3	17.8	23.7	17.9	12.0	45.5	12.9	18.0	14.5	19.8
Lublin	42.9	20.7	31.4	25.7	19.4	21.7	20.4	23.2	27.9	12.0	32.9	22.5	22.7	12.0	11.0
Katowice	62.1	19.9	18.7	25.7	19.6	37.7	22.6	13.4	24.1	12.3	54.4	14.6	18.2	26.4	22.5
Gdynia	37.0	17.7	13.4	35.9	11.3	15.5	19.6	11.8	14.8	11.0	37.4	10.4	25.0	30.1	17.6
Kielce	74.2	24.1	21.5	20.7	12.7	15.1	19.3	13.7	13.1	12.4	38.4	15.6	20.9	16.7	12.4
Min	37.0	16.4	12.4	16.1	11.3	15.1	17.8	11.8	13.1	11.0	32.9	10.4	18.0	12.0	11.0

Source: Own elaboration.

In A1 group (5 questions concerning investments), considering Question 1, the shortest average time of 37 sec. to get the answer was recorded by Gdynia (calculated for all users). With regard to Question 2, 3 and 4 the shortest average time was recorded by Krakow - 16.4 sec., 12.4 sec., 16.1 sec., accordingly. In case of Question 5, the shortest average time of 11.3 sec was recorded by Gdynia.

The second set of 5 questions was related to business (A_2 group). Considering Question 6, the shortest average time of 15.1 sec. to find an answer was reached by Kielce. With regard to Question 7 Kraków had average time of 17.8 sec., in respect to Question 8 Gdynia -11.8 sec., to Question 9 Kielce 13.1 sec., and to Question 10 Gdynia - 11.0 sec.

The third set of 5 questions considered tourism (A_3 group). With regard to Question 11 Lublin recorded time of getting the answer within 32.9 sec., considering Question 12 Gdynia - 10.4 sec., Question 13 Kraków - 18.0 sec., Question 14 Lublin - 12.0 sec., in respect to Question 15 also Lublin - 11.0 sec. Table 4.4 presents average time required to reach the answer by Polish users.

Table 4.4. Matrix A' presents average time required by Polish users.

City	Q1	Q2	Q3	Q4	Q5	Q6	Q7	Q8	Q9	Q10	Q11	Q12	Q13	Q14	Q15
		A_1' Investments					A_2 ' Business					A_3 ' Tourism			
Szczecin	94.1	55.2	38.0	55.0	49.1	54.2	34.9	25.6	46.1	40.0	46.4	25.7	39.1	24.3	27.4
Warszawa	53.8	28.0	24.8	31.7	20.4	33.0	26.8	15.3	30.1	23.2	21.1	14.1	22.7	16.5	20.6
Kraków	43.3	18.2	17.2	23.6	18.7	18.1	24.8	12.7	23.0	14.2	28.1	15.8	18.8	18.9	16.2
Łódź	42.5	21.2	17.6	14.6	15.9	15.5	14.3	10.4	17.7	17.4	31.6	13.8	11.8	11.8	11.4
Bydgoszcz	42.2	11.7	17.3	14.9	15.7	12.6	11.2	8.4	12.7	15.3	23.7	13.2	9.3	9.4	11.3
Katowice	23.1	12.0	10.1	10.2	10.5	6.9	12.7	5.9	11.1	16.2	26.9	7.6	10.5	10.7	9.9
Gdynia	24.5	12.5	12.6	11.2	10.9	6.9	10.5	5.4	9.5	8.9	21.2	9.8	8.2	12.9	5.7
Częstochowa	29.6	10.9	14.0	15.4	9.1	5.8	8.9	4.9	11.1	8.7	19.5	15.5	9.3	10.7	8.3
Min	23.1	10.9	10.1	10.2	9.1	5.8	8.9	4.9	9.5	8.7	19.5	7.6	8.2	9.4	5.7

Source: Own elaboration.

Tab. 4.4 shows that Katowice has the shortest average time to get the answer to Question 1. All tables and data concerning cities are available *in appendix on the CD* Appendices/New analysis/Polish/ average time / sheets – all cities.

Number of users who found required information within a timeframe between the shortest and the average time calculated for all the answers.

The greatest number of users who found a website including required information may prove that such a websites has better usability (easier access to information compared to other services, webpage provides more and better quality information). The number of characters on the webpage including answer was calculated. This number represents the webpage code what facilitates web-tracking system to identify a link. This data are used to design a new webpage.

Table 4.5 includes largest number of foreign users who selected the same webpage including required information within the discussed timeframe, while Table 4.6 includes information relating to Polish users. This timeframe defines time between the shortest and the average time required to find the answer to posted question, for every city. In Matrix B, B_1 group contains questions relating to investments, B_2 to business, and B_3 to tourism.

Table 4.5. Matrix B presents maximal number of foreign users who found required information within the considered timeframe or time threshold.

City	B_1 Investments					B_2 Business					B_3 Tourism				
	Q1	Q2	Q3	Q4	Q5	Q6	Q7	Q8	Q9	Q10	Q11	Q12	Q13	Q14	Q15
Poznań	7	5	6	7	12	4	2	5	2	2	7	6	4	7	5
Szczecin	2	2	3	3	3	3	2	2	2	4	2	2	2	4	3
Warszawa	6	5	4	2	3	2	2	2	2	2	3	2	5	2	8
Kraków	5	3	3	2	3	3	3	3	3	3	3	3	3	2	2
Lublin	9	6	5	9	7	7	7	5	3	4	7	11	6	10	15
Katowice	6	5	4	4	5	4	5	4	3	3	6	9	12	6	6
Gdynia	4	6	7	5	5	6	5	6	5	5	2	2	2	2	2
Kielce	7	9	8	6	9	9	9	11	8	10	11	14	14	8	5

Source: Own elaboration.

For example with regard to Question 1, 4, 14, 15, the majority of users (within the considered timeframe) found required information on Lublin website. While information relating to Questions 2, 3, 6, 7, 8, 9, 10, 11, 12 and 13, in considered timeframe was found by majority of users on Kielce website.

Table 4.6. Matrix B' presents maximal number of Polish users who found required information within the considered timeframe or time threshold.

	Matrix B'														
	B_1' Investments					B_2' Business					B_3' Tourism				
City	Q1	Q2	Q3	Q4	Q5	Q6	Q7	Q8	Q9	Q10	Q11	Q12	Q13	Q14	Q15
Szczecin	8	7	3	5	5	4	7	5	2	2	4	7	3	3	2
Warszawa	9	8	8	10	6	6	6	6	9	11	5	5	7	16	7
Kraków	8	6	8	6	6	7	6	7	8	7	4	5	4	4	5
Łódź	7	4	5	15	11	14	7	9	5	6	4	12	6	7	12
Bydgoszcz	10	7	7	7	7	7	7	10	9	7	6	6	8	5	7
Katowice	13	18	7	9	14	17	4	24	16	5	7	15	16	7	15
Gdynia	10	10	10	8	8	7	9	8	9	8	9	6	6	6	9
Częstochowa	5	4	5	5	5	5	5	5	6	5	5	5	5	5	20

Source: Own elaboration.

Table 4.6 shows frequency of finding information by users within the considered timeframe. Katowice website has higher frequency with regard to Questions 1, 2, 6, 8, 9,1 2 and 13; Warszawa website, regarding Question 10 and 14; Łódź webpage with regard to Questions 4 and 5; Gdynia webpage with regard to Questions 3, 7, 11, and Częstochowa with regard to Question 15.

Website usability can be measured by calculating minimum number of links used to reach a desired webpage. This procedure involves 3 steps. In the first one, web-tracking system calculates number of links used by every user. Data is recorded in the system database. It should be noted that some of users did not have links saved to find desired information (0 value assigned to some questions) and in some cases users needed many links to reach the answer. In the second step, data (number of links) were ordered from the highest to the smallest number. In the third step number of users who found desired information with number of clicks (in links to this information) falling within a range between the smallest and the average number of clicks calculated based all clicks, was calculated.

Number of users who found desired information with number of clicks (in links to this information) falling within a range between the smallest and the average number of clicks calculated based all clicks.

Table 4.7 presents number of foreign users and Table 4.8 number of Polish users who to find information needed from 1 to average number of links (range between the smallest number and average calculated based on all clicks). These values were calculated for every question. This is a very important ration because it measures how many users (in web-tracking system experiment) found desired information. In Matrix C, C_1 group contains questions relating to investments, C_2 to business, C_3 to tourism.

Table 4.7 Matrix C presents number of foreign users who found desired information in considered range of clicks or link threshold.

	Matrix C														
	C_1 Investments					C_2 Business					C_3 Tourism				
City	Q1	Q2	Q3	Q4	Q5	Q6	Q7	Q8	Q9	Q10	Q11	Q12	Q13	Q14	Q15
Poznań	6	12	14	12	17	10	11	7	11	5	15	7	10	14	7
Szczecin	10	13	12	15	6	6	4	6	10	5	16	6	4	10	6
Warszawa	10	7	11	10	5	8	4	5	6	4	15	7	6	5	2
Kraków	20	3	1	4	1	5	3	2	3	1	6	2	2	1	3
Lublin	7	4	12	13	8	9	16	5	9	4	19	14	10	17	2
Katowice	6	3	5	8	0	12	5	1	0	0	14	6	3	11	4
Gdynia	16	2	1	3	0	1	1	1	0	0	17	1	7	5	4
Kielce	12	3	3	3	1	4	2	1	4	4	18	3	6	11	3

Source: Own elaboration.

The best city website is the one who has the greatest number of users assigned to the considered range of links. For example, with regard to Question 1 the best website is the one of Krakow, since 20 users were assigned to the range of links in question.

Table 4.8. Matrix C' presents number of Polish users who found desired information in considered range of clicks or link threshold.

	Matrix C'														
	C_1' Investments					C_2' Business					C_3' Tourism				
City	Q1	Q2	Q3	Q4	Q5	Q6	Q7	Q8	Q9	Q10	Q11	Q12	Q13	Q14	Q15
Szczecin	23	30	25	34	27	26	31	21	32	31	35	14	25	14	26
Warszawa	41	22	25	21	14	19	26	12	25	13	26	10	22	21	19
Kraków	41	12	16	16	15	9	17	7	21	8	14	14	14	9	8

	Matrix C'														
	C_1' Investments					C_2' Business					C_3' Tourism				
City	Q1	Q2	Q3	Q4	Q5	Q6	Q7	Q8	Q9	Q10	Q11	Q12	Q13	Q14	Q15
Łódź	28	11	15	3	4	12	16	2	13	11	16	21	3	22	3
Bydgoszcz	24	18	9	18	19	5	20	2	3	17	17	13	8	12	10
Katowice	18	6	2	4	8	3	10	2	8	12	26	8	6	21	4
Gdynia	31	10	15	18	9	3	7	1	8	5	20	9	7	9	2
Częstocho-wa	29	6	20	20	1	5	6	1	6	7	21	13	7	24	7
Max	41	30	25	34	27	26	31	21	32	31	35	21	25	24	26

Source: Own elaboration.

Considering Table 4.8 the best city website will be the one who had the greatest number of users assigned to the range of used links. For example, with regard to Question 1 the best websites were the ones of Warszawa and Kraków.

Average assessment of website content quality

Website content quality is the next important factor. The users evaluated quality of information found on website while searching for answer to the question. When reaching the required information, the user assessed its quality in a range from 0 to 9 (0- poor, 9 perfect). The evaluation referred to such issues like e.g. number of information on website, ease to reach this information, time to find this information etc. Thus users assessed every website considering if it contained required information, how much information was provided and what additional service the website could offer, how much time was required to reach the information, its usability.

Table 4.9 (for foreign users) and 4.10 (for Polish users) include average values regarding information quality assessed by the users (Likert scale from 0 to 9). Data were analysed in order to calculate average quality for every question, for each city website. Matrices D, D_1 contain questions regarding investments, D_2 business and D_3 tourism area.

Table 4.9. Average assessment of website content for individual questions and cities provided by foreign users

City	Matrix D														
	D_1 Investments					D_1 Business					D_3 Tourism				
	Q1	Q2	Q3	Q4	Q5	Q6	Q7	Q8	Q9	Q10	Q11	Q12	Q13	Q14	Q15
Poznań	6.04	6.33	7.00	7.20	7.83	4.00	5.50	6.29	4.43	5.78	6.95	7.62	6.57	8.04	7.27
Szczecin	6.96	6.17	6.68	6.58	5.59	3.00	7.25	6.55	5.86	5.14	6.76	6.92	6.63	7.88	7.25
Warszawa	6.81	5.94	5.50	5.89	6.25	5.50	7.00	5.53	4.89	5.60	6.65	6.88	6.43	7.64	7.42
Kraków	3.91	4.30	5.33	4.77	4.50	4.71	4.13	4.60	4.28	5.20	6.48	6.77	6.46	7.00	6.62
Lublin	7.92	6.58	7.54	7.92	6.55	5.80	7.77	7.00	6.10	7.20	8.23	8.28	7.00	8.15	7.32
Katowice	7.33	6.88	7.29	7.00	6.47	5.25	6.40	7.00	5.94	6.25	6.72	7.35	7.05	6.41	6.91
Gdynia	5.50	4.75	4.85	4.06	4.31	4.67	4.00	4.50	4.14	5.00	6.36	6.08	5.50	5.86	5.33
Kielce	5.47	5.53	5.28	6.05	5.17	6.21	5.80	5.00	5.93	6.43	6.17	5.47	6.00	7.15	5.60
Max	7.92	6.88	7.54	7.92	7.83	6.21	7.77	7.00	6.10	7.20	8.23	8.28	7.05	8.15	7.42

Source: Own elaboration.

Table 4.9 shows that with regard to most of questions Lublin website had the higher rating compared to other cities' websites. Yet, some websites like e.g. Poznań, Warszawa, Katowice, or Kielce reached higher results considering the other questions.

Table 4.10. Average assessment of website content for individual questions and cities provided by Polish users.

City	Matrix D'														
	D_1' Investments					D_1' Business					D_1' Tourism				
	Q1	Q2	Q3	Q4	Q5	Q6	Q7	Q8	Q9	Q10	Q11	Q12	Q13	Q14	Q15
Szczecin	6.74	6.20	6.85	5.78	6.24	5.71	6.45	5.84	5.55	5.51	6.55	6.46	6.07	6.90	7.32
Warszawa	6.35	5.95	6.43	6.19	6.21	4.97	5.31	5.98	5.73	5.16	7.11	7.24	6.89	7.80	7.74
Kraków	6.19	6.29	6.18	6.35	5.86	5.50	5.80	5.96	5.90	6.47	6.91	6.86	6.52	7.03	7.04
Łódź	6.70	6.75	6.54	7.00	6.65	5.65	6.37	5.95	5.87	6.07	7.04	7.21	6.66	7.36	6.78
Bydgoszcz	6.26	6.71	6.18	6.97	6.34	6.00	6.80	5.90	6.48	5.94	6.58	6.82	5.94	7.28	6.51
Katowice	6.96	6.19	6.67	7.39	6.51	6.04	6.89	6.11	6.05	6.57	6.64	6.91	5.63	6.17	6.49
Gdynia	6.20	5.63	6.15	6.79	5.62	5.45	5.08	5.25	5.12	5.34	6.51	6.77	6.00	6.32	6.46
Częstochowa	6.04	5.56	6.05	6.60	5.87	5.88	6.06	5.41	5.72	5.58	6.23	7.24	6.00	7.64	6.46
Max	6.96	6.75	6.85	7.39	6.65	6.04	6.89	6.11	6.48	6.57	7.11	7.24	6.89	7.80	7.74

Source: Own elaboration.

Comparison included in Table 4.10 shows that with regard to content quality of websites Polish users gave highest scores to: Szczecin, Warszawa, Łódź, Bydgoszcz, Katowice and Częstochowa.

Analysis of websites usability

The next methodological step is the websites usability analysis, called FUF (Flexibility – ease to use a website, User-satisfaction – user satisfaction while browsing a website, Few errors – the level of mistakes occurred when searching for information). In this step, users, following searching and browsing of a website make their assessment in terms of FUF, using Likert scale from 0 to 9. Average FUF rates received under foreign users' assessment are presented in Table 4.11 and based on Polish users' assessment in Table 4.12.

Table 4.11. Average FUF rates for all websites provided by foreign users.

	Poznań	Szczecin	Warsza-wa	Kraków	Lublin	Katowi-ce	Gdynia	Kielce
Flexibility	6.70	6.96	6.95	6.44	8.04	7.17	6.50	5.85
User- sat-isfaction	6.46	7.00	7.13	6.33	7.42	7.00	6.20	5.70
Few errors	3.91	4.32	4.05	4.67	4.08	4.00	4.15	4.67

Source: Own elaboration.

Calculated values presented in table 4.11 show that Lublin website has the highest value for all 3 FUF parameters, while Poznan have lowest valuein few errors. Assessment was made by foreign users.

Table 4.12. Average FUF rates for all websites provided by Polish users.

	Szczecin	Warszawa	Kraków	Łódź	Bydgoszcz	Katowice	Gdynia	Często-chowa
Flexibility	6.82	7.08	7.07	7.07	6.70	6.75	6.66	6.73
User- satis-faction	7.16	6.86	6.79	6.59	6.56	6.39	6.46	5.87
Few errors	3.06	3.04	3.52	2.97	3.54	3.53	3.55	3.41

Source: Own elaboration.

Overview of results presented in Tab 4.12 shows that Warszawa website got the highest rate in Flexibility, while Szczecin website the best rating in terms User-satisfaction and Łódź the best rating in few errors. Assessment was made by Polish users.

Table 4.13 (foreign users) and 4.14 (Polish users) show the matrix containing sum of rates of individual FUF parameters.

Table 4.13. Calculated sum of FUF rates for all websites provided by foreign users.

	Poznań	Szczecin	Warsza-wa	Kraków	Lublin	Katowi-ce	Gdynia	Kielce
Flexibility	181	160	153	116	209	172	78	117
User- satisfaction	168	168	164	133	193	161	93	114
Few errors	86	95	89	84	106	88	54	70

Source: Own elaboration.

Tab. 4.13 shows FUF sum, where Lublin had the best resultand Gdyniawas the best rating in the few errors. The same calculation procedure was applied to city websites, in Polish version, visited by Polish users.

Table 4.14. Calculated sum of FUF rates for all websites provided by Polish users.

	Szczecin	Warszawa	Kraków	Łódź	Bydgoszcz	Katowice	Gdynia	Często-chowa
Flexibility	648	595	495	573	556	479	426	518
User- satisfaction	702	583	475	534	505	422	368	452
Few errors	219	231	211	217	251	219	188	218

Source: Own elaboration.

Tab. 4.14 shows that Szczecin website reached the highest place in terms of facility to use the website (Flexibility), User- satisfaction and level of mistakes made while Gdyna reached the best level of mistakes made searching for information (Few errors).

All results of assessment of Polish and English version of websites are *availablein appendix on the CD*Appendices/Original Data/new analysis/FUF-English or Polish.

4.2 Application of VMCM method to rank websites

On the basis of results included in 4.6, 4.8, 4.10, 4.12, 4.14 considering Polish users and Tables 4.5, 4.7, 4.9, 4.11, 4.13 considering foreign users, the following indicators have been calculated:

X_1 - average time required by a user to reach the relevant information,

X_2 - the largest number of users who reached desired information in the timeframe between the shortest time required (time threshold) to answer a question and average time calculated for all answers,

X_3 - number of users who found required information through clicks (in links to this information), falling in the range between the smallest number of clicks and average number (link threshold) calculated based on all clicks,

X_4 - average quality assessment made by users evaluating content of the website.

These indicators were calculated separately for every city and for each of 3 groups of information (investments, business, tourism).

Value of X_1 (for a given city) is calculated as the average of matrix A_1 (for a given group of information), by analogy X_2 is the average of matrix B_1, X_3 is the average of matrix C_1, X_4 is the average of matrix D_1.

For example, X_1 indicator (investments) is calculated according to the following formula:

$$X_1 = (1/5)*A1*1, \quad X_2=(1/5)*B1*1, \quad X_3=(1/5)*C1*1, \quad X_4=(1/5)*D1*1,$$

$$X_1 = \left(\frac{1}{5}\right) * A1 * 1 = \left(\frac{1}{5}\right) * \begin{bmatrix} a_{11} & \cdots & a_{15} \\ \vdots & \ddots & \vdots \\ a_{81} & \cdots & a_{85} \end{bmatrix} * \begin{bmatrix} 1 \\ 1 \\ 1 \\ 1 \\ 1 \end{bmatrix}$$

where:

X_1 - is a column vector of average for each city,

that is $X_1= [x_1, x_2,...,x_8]^T$.

The whole matrix $X = [X_1, X_2, X_3, X_4]$ has been calculated using the following program:

for k= 1 to 4

    fori= 1 to 8

        s=0

        for j=1 to 5

            s=s + a(j)

        next j

        b(i)= s/5

    nexti

    x(i,k)=b(i)

next k

where: k – index of vectors of X_1, X_2, X_3, X_4;

    j – index of a question 1 through 5;

    i- index of a city 1 through 8.

Table 4.15 (for foreign users) and 4.16 (for Polish users) shows the overview of all indicators for individual cities and separately for 3 groups of information (investments, business, tourism).

Table 4.15.Indicators relating to all parameters for foreign users.

City	Investments				Business				Tourists			
	X_1	X_2	X_3	X_4	X_1	X_2	X_3	X_4	X_1	X_2	X_3	X_4
Poznań	7.40	12.20	6.88	49.80	3.00	8.80	5.20	40.21	5.80	10.60	7.29	28.57
Szczecin	2.60	11.20	6.39	42.74	2.60	6.20	5.56	26.75	2.60	5.56	7.09	27.61
Warszawa	4.00	8.60	6.08	32.76	2.00	5.40	5.70	29.57	4.00	5.70	7.01	21.71
Kraków	3.20	5.80	4.56	29.35	3.00	2.80	4.58	18.94	2.60	4.58	6.67	22.12
Lublin	7.20	8.80	7.30	27.99	5.20	8.60	6.77	21.02	9.80	6.77	7.80	20.20
Katowice	4.80	4.40	6.99	29.18	3.80	3.60	6.17	22.02	7.80	6.17	6.89	27.22
Gdynia	5.40	4.40	4.69	23.08	5.40	0.60	4.46	14.53	2.00	4.46	5.83	24.07
Kielce	7.80	4.40	5.50	30.65	9.40	3.00	5.88	14.72	10.40	5.88	6.08	20.79

Source: Own elaboration.

Table 4.16.Indicators relating to all parameters for Polish users.

City	Investments				Business				Tourists			
	X_1	X_2	X_3	X_4	X_1	X_2	X_3	X_4	X_1	X_2	X_3	X_4
Szczecin	5.60	27.80	6.36	58.26	4.00	28.20	5.81	40.17	3.80	22.80	6.66	32.59
Warszawa	8.20	24.60	6.24	31.74	7.60	19.00	5.43	25.67	8.00	5.43	7.21	18.98
Kraków	6.80	20.00	6.19	24.20	7.00	12.40	5.92	18.56	4.40	5.92	6.87	19.56
Łódź	8.40	12.20	6.72	22.36	8.20	10.80	5.98	15.07	8.20	5.98	7.01	16.06
Bydgoszcz	7.60	17.60	6.49	20.38	8.00	9.40	6.22	12.03	6.40	6.22	6.63	13.38
Katowice	12.20	7.60	6.73	13.19	13.20	7.00	6.33	10.55	12.00	6.33	6.37	13.12
Gdynia	9.20	16.60	6.08	14.35	8.20	4.80	5.25	8.25	7.20	5.25	6.41	11.54
Częstochowa	4.80	15.20	6.03	15.80	5.20	5.00	5.73	7.86	8.00	5.73	6.71	12.67

Source: Own elaboration.

Further, X_1, X_2, X_3, X_4 indicators were used to build aggregate measures to evaluate websites usability:

- IM - the measure of evaluation of a website in regard to new investment with the use of X_1 - X_4

- BM- the aggregate measure of evaluation of a website in regard to already exist-ing businesses constructed with the use of X_1 - X_4

- TM – the aggregate measure of evaluation of a website in regard to people inter-ested in tourism, constructed with the use of X_1 - X_4;

- UFUF - aggregate measure of website usability evaluated by users under survey.

With the use of VMCM method and calculated indicators (Table 4.15, 4.16) 4 aggregate measures (IM, BM, TM, UFUF) have been calculated. Measures were calculated indi-vidually for each of 3 information groups (investments, business, tourism) and for usa-bility measure UFUF. Table 4.17 shows websites ranking of individual cities grouped in four clusters. This overview refers to Polish users. The table shows that Katowice web-site achieved the highest rank in two categories (investments and business), Warszawa in tourism, and Szczecin in UFUF category.

Table 4.17.Results of application of VMCM method to rank cities' websites, for Polish users.

City	Ranking			
	IM	BM	TM	UFUF
Szczecin	-0.44	-1.07	-0.82	2.30
Warszawa	0.06	-0.44	1.15	1.17
Kraków	0.12	0.37	0.23	0.08
Łódź	1.19	0.66	1.02	0.78
Bydgoszcz	0.67	0.99	0.39	0.86
Katowice	1.81	1.57	0.68	-0.11
Gdynia	0.44	0.41	0.27	-0.84
Częstochowa	0.02	0.63	0.73	0.20

Source: Own elaboration.

Table 4.18 contains ranking of websites created under results of evaluation made by foreign users. The highest rank in three categories (investments, tourism, UFUF) was assigned to Lublin, while Kielce received the highest rank in business category.

Table 4.18.Results of application of VMCM method to rank cities' websites, for foreign users.

City	Ranking			
	IM	BM	TM	UFUF
Poznań	0.34	-0.43	0.14	1.01
Szczecin	-0.11	0.19	0.13	0.92
Warszawa	0.23	0.18	0.64	0.76
Kraków	0.08	0.43	0.48	0.08
Lublin	0.81	0.67	1.29	1.72
Katowice	0.76	0.79	0.46	0.88
Gdynia	0.48	0.88	0.12	-0.97
Kielce	0.79	1.37	0.95	-0.25

Source: Own elaboration.

Table 4.19 shows websites (Polish and English versions) which gained the highest rank under calculated aggregate measures.

Table 4.19. Final websites' ranking for Polish and English versions

Language	IM	BM	TM	UFUF
Polish	Katowice=1.81	Katowice=1.57	Warsaw=1.15	Szczecin=2.30
English	Lublin=0.81	Kielce=1.37	Lublin=1.29	Lublin=1.72

Source: Own elaboration.

The best websites solutions (according to results in Table 4.19), were implemented in the referential model dedicated to LGU websites.

Thus the Polish version of a LGU website should have features of the Katowice website with respect to investments and business and Warsaw attributes with regard to tourism. Considering FUF, a website should be modelled under the Szczecin website.

With regard to English version of a model LGU website should adopt solutions provided by Lublin website in terms of investments, tourism and FUF and Lublin website with respect to few errors.

The proposed referential model of a LGU website should include the best solutions and qualities of any of analysed categories.

4.3 Architecture of the model LGU website

The model LGU website was developed on the basis of solutions presented in Chapter four. These solutions include the best parameters from analysed city websites. These are parameters which over the research procedure gained the highest scores for each question. Analysis was carried out considering three groups of information categories, namely investments, business and tourism. Two language versions were considered: Polish and English.

Home page (as well as the others) of new website was designed on the base of FUF analysis of websites available in Polish and English. Polish version of home page was developed on the basis of adopted solutions from Szczecin website (the website with the highest rank). With regard to English version there were adopted solutions specific for homepage of Lublin (the highest FUF value in research).

The layout of the homepage of a new website is presented in Fig 4.1

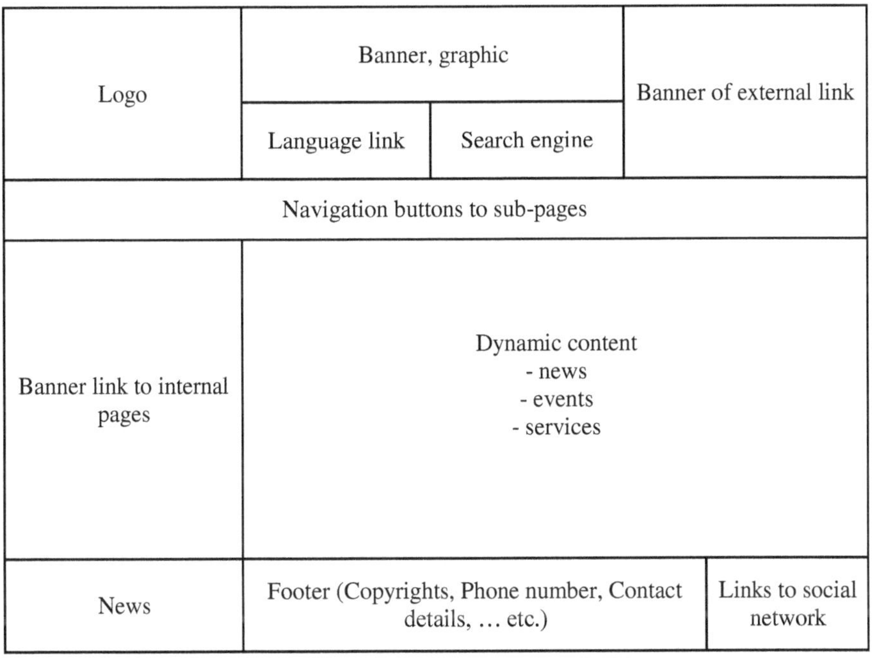

Logo	Banner, graphic		Banner of external link
	Language link	Search engine	
Navigation buttons to sub-pages			
Banner link to internal pages	Dynamic content - news - events - services		
News	Footer (Copyrights, Phone number, Contact details, ... etc.)		Links to social network

Fig. 4.1. Frame model template of the homepage of the new website.

Source: own elaboration

A frame model of the homepage includes element forming content, like: logo, language links, search engine, navigation buttons to sub–pages, banner link internal pages, dynamic content, social network links, footer copyright, contact information, and news. The choice of these elements and design were created based on the results of usability of websites. This is a very general and schematic drawing, but compliant to obtained results (Chapter 4) and includes good qualities of the best websites according to ranking.

The detailed model of the homepage, designed on the base of assumptions of the frame webpage model is presented in Fig. 4.2.

The following symbols are used on the webpage:

(1) Logo, in the working version this is the logo of University of Szczecinthe place of Author's study.

Fig. 4.2. Detailed model of the homepage of the new website, English version

Source: own elaboration

(2) The navigation button in horizontal layout, showing three showing 3 basic options: Investment, Business, and Tourism as well as additional options like: Home, News, and Contact.

(3) The navigation button in vertical layout displays the same factors as in the horizontal header (Investment, Business, and Tourism) as well as some important links. They were added there to facilitate foreign investors to become familiar with the local law and important departments of city hall and to display interesting issues relating to investments or tourism.

(4) Content includes some of attractive pictures and links to detailed content.

(5) Special offer includes a form where one may enter own e-mail or subscribe a newsletter.

(6-8) Special website areas include brief information about Investment Services, Business Centre Club, Business Opportunity. These elements were incorporated to the homepage to enhance its attractiveness.

(9) Help, allows the user to get additional information about , support , FAQ, etc.

(10) More information, provides additional groups of information e.g. contact with webmaster.

(11) Footer, contains copyright information for the website.

While creating the new version of the webpage for LGU, the author mainly focused on usability and creative qualities like: language, search engine, internal navigation tools, advanced technology, methodological recommendations, interactive tools, links and information content.

Suggested solutions to be implemented in a template of the LGU webpage should provide the users with better information content, shorter time to get the information at the same using less number of links. Satisfying of such criteria facilitate to reach the website the higher rank than those of other cities.

The website map is a way of providing a website structure in order to show how the web - based information services are organized on the website. This facilitates faster navigation; allow understanding limits in information content, identifying new information. Thus it may help to increase usability, decrease frustration and support quality of information for the new website. The structure of new website consists of four main levels. Level one includes homepage (Home). The second level includes nine internal and external links: city hall, matters, city council, local law, other entities, Szczecin investments, investment opportunities, business, tourism and contact. The third level includes 45 five links and lever four includes 23 both internal and external links.

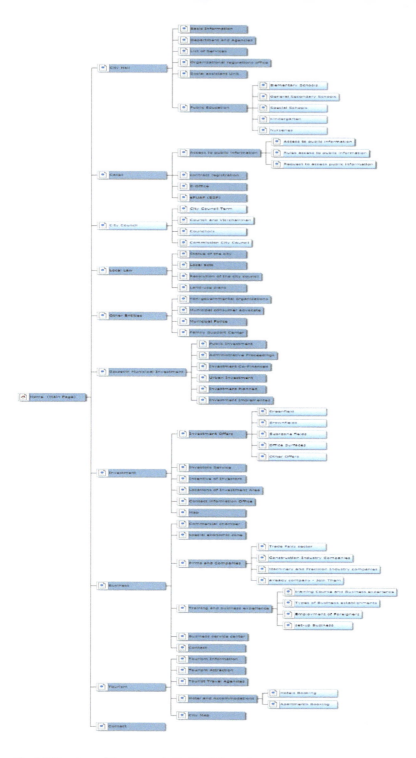

Fig. 4.3.Structure of the new website, English version.

Source: own elaboration

Well-developed structure of information organization translates into success in access to information desired by user. This allows the users to expect where required information can be found and provide resources in a systematic and efficient manner. Users that meet illogical arrangement of information or in a different layout (which the user was used to), have difficulties in using the website.

Based on the worked out design solution in the scope of information architecture (structure of information organization, web page models) fully operational, website was created, as the proposal of a template of LGU website.

Figure 4.4 represents the view of a designed homepage of a new website in English version.

Fig. 4.4. Homepage of the new website developed in English.

Source: own elaboration

Fig 4.5 shows the homepage of the new website developed in Polish.

Fig. 4.5. Homepage of the new website developed in English.
Source: own elaboration

At the top of the homepage of the new website there is the header including links to important sections that is to investments, business and tourism area. On the left site there are links to selected sub-pages.

The layout of the sub-page relating to investments is presented in Fig 4.6. Content of this website includes among the others links to webpages presenting investment opportunities, incentives for investors, location of area to invest, information office, maps.

Fig. 4.6. Sub-page of the new website related to investments , developed in English.

Source: own elaboration

Polish version of the subpage dedicated to investments is presented in Fig. 4.7.

Fig. 4.7. Sub-page of the new website related to investments, developed in Polish

Source: own elaboration

Fig. 4.8.shows the exemplary webpage of „Investment Offers", as the sub-page to the page relating to investments (sub-link of investment webpage).

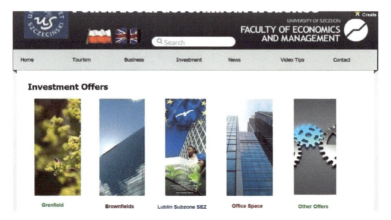

Fig. 4.8. Sub-page relating to investment offers developed in English.

Source: own elaboration

Webpage including investment offers was developed according to solutions adopted from the analogous webpage of Lublin website.

The webpage dedicated to issue concerning business (in English versions) was designed according to guidelines of Kielce website in English version (Fig. 4.9).

Fig. 4.9. Sub-page relating to business, developed inEnglish.

Source: own elaboration

From the level of this webpage one can access information on chambers of commerce, special economic zones, companies, experience in education or business, business services centres or contact. The webpage includes also two pictures operating as links, reassigns to information required by businessmen. Fig 4.10 shows the webpage including content of the first link selected from menu level (Chamber of Commerce).

Fig. 4.10. The webpage dedicated to Chambers of Commerce, in English version.

Source: own elaboration

The webpage concerning the Chambers of Commerce (English version) was also designed following Kielce specifications. There are external and internal links to detailed information. Provision of balance among site components seemed to be necessary as well. The user perceives it as a set of many elements present on the webpage (text, graphic) but when these elements are ordered the effect of clarity is visible. User can easy find required information there.

Figure 4.11 shows the Polish version of the webpage dedicated to business and Fig. 4.12 Polish version of the webpage including information about the chamber of commerce.

Fig. 4.11. Webpage dedicated to business developed in Polish

Source: own elaboration

Fig. 4.12. Webpage dedicated to Chamber of Commerce developed in Polish version of website.

Source: own elaboration

Webpages dedicated to tourism have been presented in Fig 4.13 (English version) and in Fig. 4.14 (Polish version).

Fig. 4.13. Webpage dedicated to tourism, developed in English.
Source: own elaboration

Fig. 4.14. Webpage dedicated to tourism, developed in Polish.
Source: own elaboration

Sub-pages of section relating to tourism including information about Tourist Information Offices are presented in Fig. 4.15 (English version) and4.16 (Polish version).

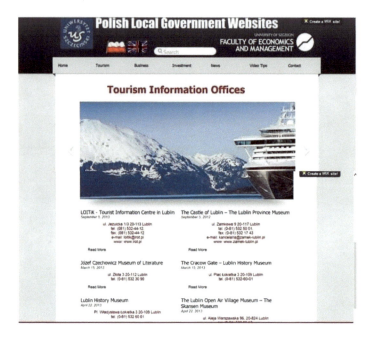

Fig. 4.15. Webpage including information about Tourist Information Offices developed in English.

Source: own elaboration

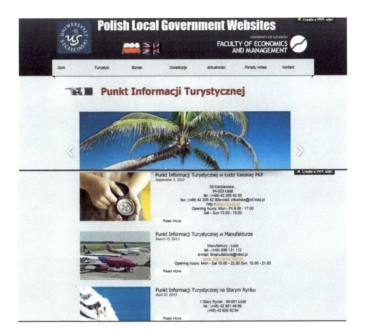

Fig. 4.16. Webpage including information about Tourist Information Offices developed in Polish.

Source: own elaboration

5. VERIFICATION AND ASSESMENT OF THE PROPOSED SOLUTION

On the basis of a developed referential model of LGU website the proposal of a model LGU website has been made. Then for such developed model website analysis aiming at verification of assumed solutions with regard to the proposed structure and information content has been repeated. On the base of conducted experiment with the use of the web-tracking system parameters like e.g.: average time to answer the question; number of people who found required information within the defined timeframe; number of clicks in links to this information; average assessment of the website content quality have been calculated. The results obtained for the model LGU website have been then compared to results obtained for 8 analysed city websites. The last stage of research concerned usability analysis FUF for the model LGU website and comparison of these results to previous results of individual cities. In case the model website achieved better results it would prove the rightness of assumed solutions.

In experiments regarding model design of LGU website 12 foreign and 10 Polish users took part. By analogy to the previous studies were to provide answers to 15 questions (perform tasks).

First, time required to find the answer to a given question by each of the users was subject to analysis. Then the average time required to find the answer to every question was calculated. Results for foreign users are presented in Table 5.1 (U means a user, Q means a question).

Table 5.1.Time and average time required by foreign users to obtain answer, calculated for new service.

No	Q1	Q2	Q3	Q4	Q5	Q6	Q7	Q8	Q9	Q10	Q11	Q12	Q13	Q14	Q15
U1	12	13	10	18	10	10	11	14	12	11	29	9	12	10	16
U2	42	11	12	17	11	17	8	8	13	12	31	8	14	12	8
U3	41	12	9	18	13	8	7	8	8	5	29	11	22	8	9
U4	33	12	8	14	12	8	8	9	4	5	24	10	20	8	10
U5	23	32	14	19	9	9	8	11	5	7	22	11	18	7	12
U6	22	14	8	18	7	7	10	10	7	10	20	10	17	12	11
U7	15	15	7	14	8	8	10	7	10	11	17	8	12	15	10
U8	16	12	9	19	8	10	22	7	5	14	15	8	15	14	11

No	Q1	Q2	Q3	Q4	Q5	Q6	Q7	Q8	Q9	Q10	Q11	Q12	Q13	Q14	Q15
U9	20	20	14	17	12	12	17	8	12	10	14	9	13	11	7
U10	33	19	9	15	12	20	13	12	16	12	14	10	12	10	7
U11	31	19	14	10	10	14	10	10	16	9	10	11	14	9	6
U12	23	7	10	8	9	5	9	14	9	9	9	8	11	6	5
Avearge	25.9	15.5	10.3	15.6	10.1	10.7	11.1	9.8	9.8	9.6	19.5	9.4	15.0	10.2	9.3

Source: Own elaboration.

Collected results (Tab. 5.1) have been compared to matrix A, including average time required for answer to the given question calculated for the individual cities by foreign users (Tab. 4.3). Chart 5.1 represents values of the average time required to answer questions obtained for model website and city websites subject to previous analysis.

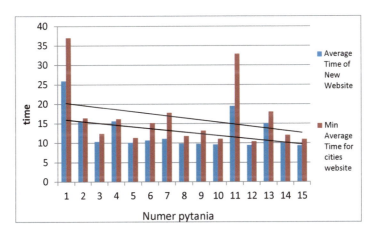

Chart 5.1. Comparison between the average time required to answer question calculated for the new service and minimum average time on cities' websites calculated for foreign users
Source: Own elaboration.

Bar charts show differences between the average times: blue bar means average time required for answer to questions for the new website and red bar means minimal average time for city websites. Calculated time for answer for new website developed in English are shorter than those of existing cities.

The same procedure was repeated for the design of the service in Polish version. Table 5.2 shows answers received from the web-tracking system.

Table 5.2. Time required for answer, obtained on model website by Polish users.

No	Q1	Q2	Q3	Q4	Q5	Q6	Q7	Q8	Q9	Q10	Q11	Q12	Q13	Q14	Q15
U1	16	9	8	6	11	6	9	5	10	10	12	9	9	10	7
U2	15	10	9	11	7	7	4	4	7	9	10	8	8	9	5
U3	15	11	10	8	8	7	8	6	7	9	14	9	5	9	6
U4	11	9	9	10	7	4	10	5	9	7	9	8	9	9	4
U5	26	12	11	8	9	5	9	4	8	8	9	5	5	8	4
U6	21	9	14	11	10	5	5	6	8	10	10	6	8	7	7
U7	22	9	14	10	11	6	8	6	10	9	11	5	7	6	3
U8	11	6	5	9	7	7	7	4	5	5	15	8	9	11	6
U9	14	7	8	5	6	4	8	3	6	7	13	7	10	10	4
U10	19	8	7	9	8	5	7	3	7	8	9	8	8	6	4
Average	17	9	9.5	8.7	8.4	5.6	7.5	4.6	7.7	8.2	11.2	7.3	7.8	8.5	5

Source: Own elaboration.

Chart 5.2 illustrates the comparision between the avearge time for answer obtained on the model website (Tab 5.2) and the average time required for answer on discussed websites, coming from A' matrix (Tab. 4.4).

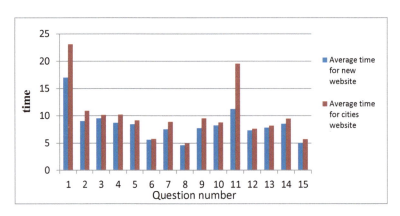

Chart 5.2.Comparison between the average time for answer obtained on the model website and the minimum average time required for answer on discussed websites, for Polish users.

Source: Own elaboration.

Chart 5.2 shows difference between the new and the other websites for Polish users in terms of average time required to find the answer. Time for answer became shorter compared to webpages of previously considered cities.

Average assessment of web content quality

Next step relied on comparison of web content quality between the new model website and the former websites. Users made quality assessment of information contained on the websites in a range from 0-9. Table 5.3 shows evaluations of individual users for the subsequent questions. There were calculated averages of user's assessments, which will be used in comparison with average information quality assessment on websites made in previous stage of research (evaluation of city websites). The assessment results have been provided by foreign users.

Table 5.3.Assessment of web content quality on webpages of the new site made by foreign users.

No	Q1	Q2	Q3	Q4	Q5	Q6	Q7	Q8	Q9	Q10	Q11	Q12	Q13	Q14	Q15
U1	9	9	9	9	9	9	9	9	9	9	9	9	9	9	9
U2	9	9	9	9	9	9	9	9	9	9	9	9	9	9	9
U3	9	9	9	9	9	9	9	9	9	9	9	9	9	9	9
U4	9	9	9	9	9	9	9	9	9	9	9	9	9	9	9
U5	9	9	9	9	9	9	8	9	9	9	9	9	9	9	9
U6	8	8	8	9	9	9	8	8	9	9	9	9	9	9	9
U7	8	8	8	9	9	9	8	8	8	9	9	9	9	9	9
U8	8	8	8	8	8	9	8	8	8	9	9	9	9	9	9
U9	7	8	8	8	8	8	8	6	8	9	8	8	8	9	9
U10	7	7	8	8	8	8	8	6	8	8	8	8	8	8	9
U11	7	7	8	8	7	7	8	6	8	7	8	8	8	7	8
U12	7	6	8	7	7	7	7	0	7	6	7	7	7	7	8
Average	8.08	8.08	8.42	8.50	8.42	8.50	8.25	7.25	8.42	8.50	8.58	8.58	8.58	8.58	8.83

Source: Own elaboration.

Comparison of results in Table 5.3 to results obtained in assessment of information quality on previously analysed websites of cities (Tab 4.9) shows that for all considered issues (posed questions), the proposed template of the website is better assessed (Chart 5.3).

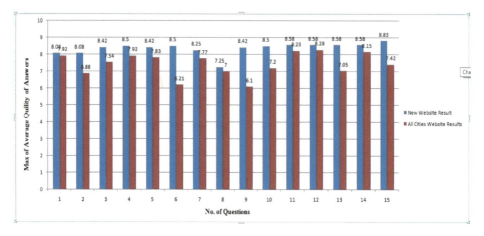

Chart 5.3.Comparison of the average quality for the new, model website and average quality of answers on city webpages (foreign users).

Source: Own elaboration.

The Polish version of the proposed website (model), the similar analysis of assessment of information quality was performer. The assessment results delivered by Polish users are presented in Table 5.4.

Table 5.4.Information quality assessment on webpages of the new website provided by Polish users.

No	Q1	Q2	Q3	Q4	Q5	Q6	Q7	Q8	Q9	Q10	Q11	Q12	Q13	Q14	Q15
U1	9	9	9	9	9	9	9	9	9	9	9	9	9	9	9
U2	9	9	9	9	9	9	9	8	8	9	9	9	9	9	9
U3	9	9	9	9	9	9	9	7	8	9	9	9	8	9	9
U4	9	9	9	9	8	9	9	7	9	9	9	9	8	9	9
U5	9	8	9	9	8	9	9	7	7	9	9	9	7	9	9
U6	6	5	9	9	7	9	9	6	9	9	9	9	7	8	8
U7	7	4	8	8	6	9	9	5	6	9	8	9	5	8	8
U8	6	4	7	8	6	7	9		5	8	8	8	4	8	7
U9	6	6	6	5	7	7	7		5	7	8	7		7	6
U10	7		6	5	6	4	7			5	4	3		6	6
Average	7.70	7.00	8.10	8.00	7.50	8.10	8.60	7.00	7.33	8.30	8.20	8.10	7.13	8.20	8.00

Source: Own elaboration.

Data included in Table 5.4 have been used to compare with data coming from information quality assessment on websites of cities (Tab. 4.10). Similarly as in case of English version proposed website model was of better assessed in context of all 15 questions (Chart 5.4).

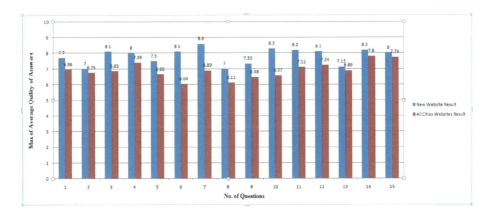

Chart 5.4.Comparison of the average information quality assessment for the new model website and average quality of answer on cities' websites (Polish users).

Source: Own elaboration.

Both in case of website version dedicated to foreign and Polish users the model website has been better evaluated in all categories (15 questions).

The next criterion for comparison of the new website to results coming from websites of already assessed cities was number of links to reach the page where the desired information was found.

Table 5.5 includes comparison of links to reach desired content. Research results refer to the users and the values are averaged.

Tab. 5.5.Average number of links used by foreign users on new website and on websites of cities in question.

	Q1	Q2	Q3	Q4	Q5	Q6	Q7	Q8	Q9	Q10	Q11	Q12	Q13	Q14	Q15
City websites	6	6	6	6	4	6	6	4	6	5	6	4	4	4	6
New website	3	1	4	2	1	1	3	2	3	2	4	4	3	2	2

Source: Own elaboration.

Chart 5.5 illustrates visually differences in number of links to find a specific information.

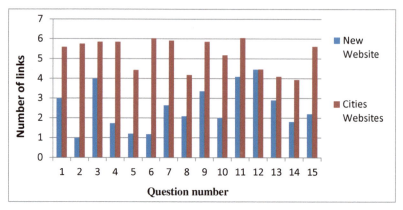

Chart 5.5.Comparison of the average number of link use by foreign users and city web-sites.Source: Own elaboration.

In each case, the new developed, redesigned website allows for quicker reach the desired content (using smaller number of links).

Analogous analyses have been performed for Polish version of the new website and websites of the individual cities. Averaged values including number of links necessary to get the answer to 15 questions (finding specific information) are presented in Table 5.6.

Table 5.6. Average number of links used on the new website and on cities' webpages (Polish users).

	Q1	Q2	Q3	Q4	Q5	Q6	Q7	Q8	Q9	Q10	Q11	Q12	Q13	Q14	Q15
New page	4	4	4	3	4	3	4	2	4	1	5	4	5	2	2
Cities websites	5	5	5	4	5	4	5	4	5	5	8	5	5	5	5

Source: Own elaboration.

The new version of the website dedicated to LGU has smaller values (except for question 13, where the same values were received), what means improvement in accessibility to desired information. Chart 5.6 provides the graphic illustration of this comparison.

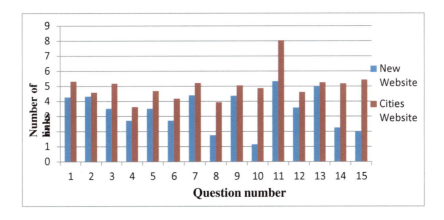

Chart 5.6.Comparison of the average number of links used by Polish users on the new website and websites of the cities.

Source: Own elaboration.

The website where the user need the smaller number of links (less clicks) can be considered as more user-friendly. A tag assigned to link should be legible and comprehensible, so that the user would not waste time to think about what it means and what content he/or she will receive by clicking in the link. Moreover links to other pages should be properly exposed, e.g. the user should be aware which of these links refer to external pages (outside website). These are basic assumptions of design of information architecture for websites and results of analysis prove that proposed model of LGU website meet these requirements.

Discussion of results (case study)

The next step was usability analysis FUF (Flexibility – ease to use a website, User-satisfaction, Few errors – level of mistakes made while searching for information) of the proposed model website for LGU. Users, (foreign and Polish) made evaluation of the new website in terms of FUF, using Likert scale from 0 to 9.

The average FUF values obtained in web-tracking system based on evaluation by foreign users are presented in Table 5.7.

Tab. 5.7 The average FUF values for the new website provided by foreign users.

	Flexibility	User- satisfaction	Few errors
Average	8.44	8.55	3.35

Source: Own elaboration.

Then obtained results (Tab. 5.7) were compared with the average FUF parameters calculated in previous step for websites of individual cities (Tab. 4.11). Comparisons relating to English versions, performed by foreign users were illustrated in Charts 5.7, 5.8, 5.9. All data resource can be found in CD/appendices/ FUF new website.

Chart 5.7 presents difference in value of Flexibility (ease to use a website). This FUF parameter has achieved greater value in case of the new website than in case of websites of cities in question.

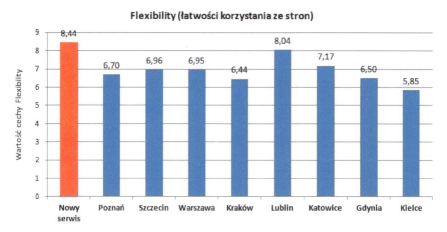

Chart 5.7.Differences between average value of Flexibility (ease to use a website) parameter of websites and the new website version (foreign users).

Source: Own elaboration.

Chart 5.8 illustrates differences in values of User-Satisfaction (Users' satisfaction in using a website) parameter. Values obtained for this parameter for the new website have greater values than in case of websites of the analysed cities.

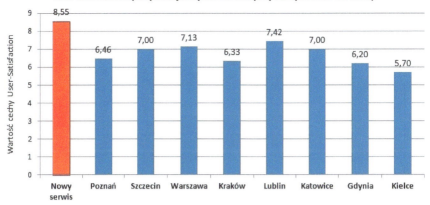

Chart 5.8.Differences between the average value of User-Satisfaction (Users' satisfaction in using a website) parameter of analysed cities' websites and the new website version (foreign users).

Source: Own elaboration.

The comparison including the level of made mistakes (Few Errors), which is connected with searching for information process, and in fact with problems, which arise is presented in Chart 5.9. Also in this case better results are noticed with regard to the new website. Better means lower values.

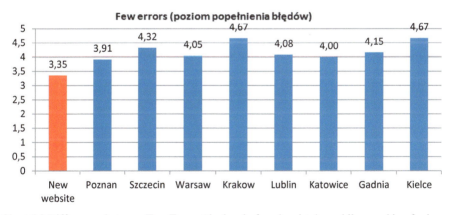

Chart 5.9.Differences between Few Errors (the level of made mistakes while searching for information) parameter of cities' websites and the new website model (foreign users).

Source: Own elaboration.

In conclusion, the new model version of the website get better assessment in terms of FUF usability than any of the previously considered website of the individual city.

The same assessment and comparison of FUF usability procedure was carried out for Polish versions of the website. Research involved Polish users.

Average FUF values obtained in web-tracking system from Polish users were presented in Table 5.8.

Tab. 5.8 Average FUF values for the new website provided by Polish users.

	Flexibility	User- satis- faction	Few errors
Average	8.40	9.00	2.35

Source: Ownelaboration.

Results presented in Tab 5.8 were compared with average values of FUF parameters calculated in the previous step for webpages of individual cities (Tab 4.12). Comparisons for Polish users were illustrated in Charts 5.10, 5.11, 5.12.

As it is visible in Chart 5.10 value obtained for Flexibility (ease in website use) parameter, in case of Polish version of the new website get greater values than in case of websites of cities in question.

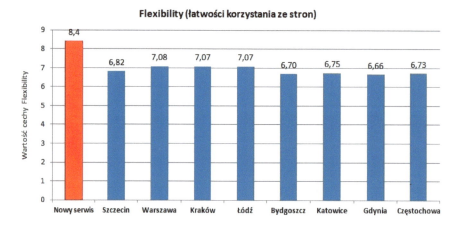

Chart 5.10. Differences between the average value of Flexibility (ease to use website) parameter of analysed webpages cities and the new version of website (Polish users).

Source: Own elaboration.

Chart 5.11 illustrates differences between values of User-Satisfaction (user satisfaction in using a website) parameter. Received values of this parameter for the Polish version of the website have greater values than in case of websites of discussed cities.

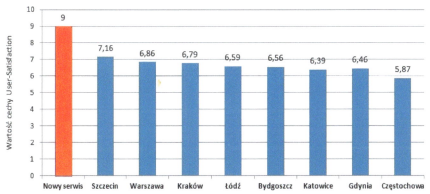

Chart 5.11.Differences between the average value of User-Satisfaction (user satisfaction in using a website) parameter of websites of the cities and the new version of the website (Polish users).

Source: Own elaboration.

Chart 5.12 illustrates values of Few Errors (level of made mistakes while searching) parameters. As it is visible, values for the new service (model website for LGU) are lower than in case of services of the analysed cities.

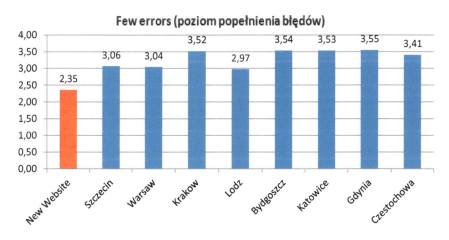

Chart 5.12.Differences between the average value of Few Errors (level of made mistakes while searching) parameter for cities' websites and the new version of the website (Polish users).

Source: Own elaboration.

CONCLUSION

The main purpose of the dissertation was to create a referential model of an LGU website with content appropriate for the needs of local and foreign users.

On the basis of empirical research of the existing Polish LGU websites, with regard to usability of these websites and for selected groups of users (citizens, people interested in visiting the city for pleasure or education and investors), especially foreign users, a referential model has been created which can form the basis of LGU website design. This model includes information architecture of a typical LGU website (structure of information outline, labelling model, navigation) as well as a proposal of highly detailed pattern of an LGU website.

On the basis of proposed model a typical LGU website has been created which includes necessary information for every Local Government Unit. This website has been re-examined by users to check its usability. Comparison of results from this work with results of previous examination of websites has shown that the current solution ensures faster access to selected information than that of previous solutions. Consequently, the purpose of this work has been achieved.

Detailed aim of this work regarding analysis of LGU service usability has been achieved through analysis of twenty selected city websites (in English and Polish). Out of twenty websites, on the basis of taxonomy method (aggregate measures), eight websites have been chosen as the most representative ones (they best fulfilled the criteria posted in the research). On the basis of selected LGU websites a solution has been created for LGU (implementation of the main objective).

Creation of webtracking software was the second detailed aim of this work and it has been fully achieved. The software enables analysis of the time and access path to information desired by the user. On the basis of implemented rules the software allows to examine the shortest access path to information, the smallest number of clicks and examination of website quality on the basis of questions answered by users for the purpose of this research.

The results of research on the existing LGU websites and research on the website created by the author have verified the stated hypothesis. The solution provides methodological clues which can be used for LGU website design. They can also be used in modification and optimization of already existing solutions. When using the proposed referential model one can design LGU websites with increased usability when compared to currently existing websites. By using the proposed referential model LGU websites of higher usability, compared to actually existing Internet solutions can be designed.

This work is an attempt to assist the websites developers' and designers' to satisfy the requirements of both the local government in one side and the group of investors, businessmen, and tourists in the other side.

The goal of this research was to assess the quality of Polish cities' websites and to understand how web-based information content is produced for Polish local governments' websites, to ensure Polish and foreign citizens both enjoy fair and equal access to governmental information. The research significance stems from the Polish local governments' daily e- service, put in place to deliver government information to citizens which raise the demand to assess the quality of this service. The research process started in the beginning of 2011, and the study passed through a number of stages to achieve its intended objectives.

The author started by surveying previous research studies on the performance of local government website implementation worldwide. Studies of developed countries' website usage aided in forming the conceptual framework for the implementation of local government websites. The author decided to conduct an exploratory study to understand the current provision delivery mechanism of government information in Poland.

The first part of the exploratory study aimed to assess the availability of government information on Polish cities' websites. This part of the study suggested that it is convenient to divide information provided into nine fields: Education, Tourism, Hotels, Restaurants, Transport, Accommodation, Business, Health and Investment. The study also suggested that the government information dispensed focus on three factors of priority: Investment, Business, and Tourism. Classifying information based on these priorities should help web developers and designers to provide the information citizens prefer to receive.

The second part of the exploratory study aimed to investigate the extent to which government information on the Polish cities' websites was accessible easily. The author investigated the implication of the use of web-tracking systems to enhance the dispensing of government information.

The author decided to develop a conceptual web-based information content assessment framework. The main framework components were website on the government information availability, web-based information quality, website usability and website accessibility.

The author developed a questionnaire based on the conceptual framework to explore citizens' preferences regarding web-based government information. The findings of this questionnaire helped the author construct the evaluation checklist used to assess the web-based content of the Polish cities' websites. The results were obtained from web-tracking system to evaluate content that meets citizens' needs on the Polish cities' websites and by using vector measure to extract the ranking of cities in each factor (investment, Business, and Tourism).

At this stage, the conceptual frameworks were improved based on citizens' preferences gained from the web-tracking results. The improved conceptual framework was reconstructed in the form of a checklist used to evaluate the local government websites. New websites have been built based on the elements that gained the best scores for each question in each city. The investigation of success of the new website which has been created was by using verification of data which obtained from web-tracking system and has been repeating the same procedure of analysis data for the new website and compare with all best features of other websites.

The author conducted experiments in 2013, and the results show substantial difference between the new website and those of all the other cities addressed to Polish users.The difference in favour to the new website. At the same the thesis objectives have been achieved.

The following aspects in this work should be considered as novelty:

- creation of the webtracking system to test websites usability of local government units. The system is designed to test websites in terms of three information categories: investment, business, tourism,

- definition of criteria to evaluate websites of local government units based on questioning both users coming from various countries and Polish experts,

- development of aggregated measures (IM, BM, TM, UFUF) as the result of adopting VMCM method, constituting basis for websites of local government units in respect of website content,

- proposal of the referential model of local government units, where the best parameters of the existing (analysed) websites of Polish cities and solutions, which are the effect of usability testing using webtracking system have been implemented.

Solutions elaborated in this dissertation may be subject to further development.

One of proposals refers to implementation of the standardized mechanisms of notification (e-mail, SMS) about new initiatives regarding investments, prospective business partners interested to establish cooperation or issues related to tourism.

The second one is related to integration between local government websites and social media (Twitter, Facebook etc.)

Another proposal concerns the use of the eyetracking system to test eye activity of LGU websites' users and based on these studies development of solutions regarding useful content arrangement on these websites.

LIST OF FIGURES

LIST OF CHARTS

site (Polish users).

LIST OF TABLES

BIBLIOGRAPHY

1) Ahn T., Ryu S.& Han I. (2007). The impact of Web quality and playfulness on user acceptance of online retailing. Information & Management.

2) Akkaya C., Obermeier M., Wolf P.& Krcmar H. (2011). Components of trust influencing egovernment adoption in Germany. Springer Berlin Heidelberg., In Electronic Government.

3) Al-Badi A. H.& Mayhew P. J. (2010). A framework for designing usable localised business websites. Communications of the IBIMA.

4) Albert W., & Tullis T. (2013). Measuring the user experience: collecting, analyzing, and presenting usability metrics. Newnes, books.google.com.

5) Alias E. S., Idris S. H., Ashaari N. S.& Kasimin, H. (2011). Evaluating e-government services in Malaysia using the EGOVSAT model. IEEE, International Conference on Electrical Engineering and Informatics (ICEEI).

6) Alshaali S. (2011). Human-Computer Interaction: Lessons from Theory and Practice. Thesis for the degree of Doctor of Philosophy. UK: UNIVERSITY OF SOUTHAMPTON,School of Management.

7) Avraham E.& Eran, K. (2008.). Media strategies for marketing places in crisis: Improving the image of cities, countries, and tourist destinations. Elsevier, Oxford, UK, Routledge.

8) Baecker R. M. (2014). Readings in Human-Computer Interaction: toward the year 2000. Morgan Kaufmann.

9) Baland J. M., Moene K. O.& Robinson J. A. (2010). Governance and development. Oslo, Norway: Published by North Holland, Handbook of development economics.

10) Banati H., Bedi P.& Grover P. S. (2006). Evaluating web usability from the user's perspective. Journal of Computer Science.

11) Baqir M. N.& Iyer L. (2010). E-government maturity over 10 Years: A comparative analysis of e-government maturity in select countries around the world. . Springer New York. In Comparative E-Government.

12) Barnes S.& Vidgen R. (2006). Data triangulation and web quality metrics: A case study in e-government. Information & Management,

13) Barnes S. & Vidgen R. (2005). The eQual Approach to the Assessment of E-Commerce Quality: A Longitudinal Study of Internet Bookstores. Web Engineering: Principles and Techniques. Idea Group Publishing.

14) Barnes S.& Vidgen, R. (2000). WebQual: An Exploration of Web Site Quality. Proceedings of the Eighth European Conference on Information Systems ECIS.

15) Batley S. (2007). The I in information architecture: the challenge of content management. In R. McGuinness (Ed.), Aslib Proceedings. Emerald Group Publishing Limited.

16) Bhuiyan M. S. (2011). Public sector eService development in Bangladesh: Status, prospects and challenges. Electronic Journal of e-Government.

17) Bilsel R. U., Büyüközkan, G.& Ruan, D. (2006). A fuzzy preference-ranking model for a quality evaluation of hospital web sites. International Journal of intelligent system.

18) Boiko B. (2005). Content Management Bible. In B. Boiko, Content Management Bible. Indianapolis, Indiana, USA: Wiley Publishing, Inc.

19) Boley B. B., McGehee N. G., Perdue R. R.& Long, P. (2014). Empowerment and resident attitudes toward tourism: Strengthening the theoretical foundation through a Weberian lens. Elsevier, Annals of Tourism Research.

20) Brzezinski Z. (2009). The choice: Global domination or global leadership. Basic Books.

21) Bouch A., Kuchinsky A.& Bhatti N. (2000). Quality is in the eye of the beholder: meeting users' requirements for Internet quality of service. ACM.,In Proceedings of the SIGCHI conference on Human Factors in Computing Systems.

22) Bueyuekoezkan G. & Ruan. D. (2007). Evaluating government websites based on a fuzzy multiple criteria decision-making approach. International Journal of Uncertainty, Fuzziness and Knowledge-Based Systems.

23) Bulkeley H. & Kern K. (2006). Local government and the governing of climate change in Germany and the UK. . Urban Studies.

24) Cao J., Crews J. M., Nunamaker J. F., BurgoonJ. K.& Lin M. (2004). User experience with Agent99 Trainer: A usability study. IEEE,In System Sciences, 2004. Proceedings of the 37th Annual Hawaii International Conference.

25) Cao M., Zhang Q. & Seydel J. (2005). B2C e-commerce web site quality: an empirical examination. . Industrial Management & Data Systems, Emerald.

26) Cappel J. J. & Huang Z. (2007). A usability analysis of company websites. Journal of Computer Information Systems.

27) Carter L. & Bélanger F. (2005). The utilization of e-government services: citizen trust, innovation and acceptance factors. Wiley Online Library, Information systems journal.

28) CastellsM. (2008). European cities, the informational society, and the global economy. Wiley Online Library, Tijdschrift voor economische en sociale geografie , Volume 84, Issue 4.

29) Caulfield J.& Larsen H. O. (2013). Local government at the millenium. Springer Science & Business Media.

30) Chen C., Wang P., Liu, Y., Wu G.& Wang P. (2013). Impacts of government website information on social sciences and humanities in China: A citation analysis. . Elsevier, Government Information Quarterly.

31) Chen Y. C.& Thurmaier K. (2008). Advancing E-Government: Financing Challenges and Opportunities. . Public Administration Review.

32) Chiou W. C., Lin C. C.& Perng C. (2010). A strategic framework for website evaluation based on a review of the literature from 1995–2006. Elsevier, Information & management.

33) Chmielarz W. (2008c). Badanie użyteczności internetowych witryn sklepów komputerowych przy pomocy metody punktowej,. Fenomen Internetu, Uniwersytet Szczeciński.

34) Chmielarz W. (2013). Comparative Analysis of Selected Websites of Brokerage Houses in Poland. . Interdisciplinary Perspectives on Business Convergence, Computing, and Legality, 10.

35) Chmielarz W. (2008). Metodyki oceny serwisów internetowych urzędów miejskich-dyskusja możliwości zastosowań. . Prace Naukowe/Akademia Ekonomiczna w Katowicach.

36) Chmielarz W. (2008a). Ocena użyteczności internetowych witryn sklepów komputerowych. Studia i materiały Polskiego Stowarzyszenia Zarządzania Wiedzą, Tom 13.

37) Chmielarz W., Szumski, O.& Zborowski, M. (2011). Kompleksowe metody ewaluacji jakości serwisów internetowych. Wydawnictwo Naukowe Wydziału Zarządzania Uniwersytetu Warszawskiego.

38) Chu R. (2001). What online Hong Kong travelers look for on airline/travel websites? International Journal of Hospitality Management.

39) Cohen L., Manion L., & Morrison K. (2007). Research Methods in Education, pp1-657,p160. London: Routledge Falmer,ISBN 0-203-02905-4.

40) Connell A. (2008). Professional SharePoint 2007 Web Content Management Development: Building Publishing Sites with Office SharePoint Server 2007. USA: John Wiley & Sons.

41) Creswell J. W. (2013). Research design: Qualitative, quantitative, and mixed methods approaches. . London: Sage Publications, Inc.

42) Cummings T.& Christopher W. (2014). Organization development and change. Cengage learning.

43) Czerwiński A.& Krzesaj M. (2014). Wybrane zagadnienia oceny jakości systemu informacyjnego w sieci WWW. Studia i Monografie/Uniwersytet Opolski.

44) Dada D. (2006). The failure of e-government in developing countries: A literature review. . The Electronic Journal of Information Systems in Developing Countries.

45) Demczuk A. & Pawłowska A. (2006). Progress toward e-government in Poland: Issues and dilemmas. . Information Polity.

46) Detlor B., Hupfer M. E., Ruhi U.& Zhao L. (2013). Information quality and community municipal portal use. Government Information Quarterly, a DeGroote School of Business.

47) Dodge Y. (2008). The concise encyclopedia of statistics. . Berlin: Springer Science & Business Media.

48) Dover D.& Dafforn E. (2011). Search engine optimization (SEO) secrets. Canada: Wiley publishing.

49) Drożyński T.& Urbaniak W. (2011). The role of local government units in supporting foreign investors in the Lodz region. Lodz, Poland: European Union under the European Social Fund. Lodz.

50) Drüke H. (2004). Concluding remarks on national specifics and transfer and adoption of good practice. Local Electronic Government.

51) Dunleavy P., Margetts H., John S.& McCarthy D. (1999). Government on the Web. LONDON: National Audit Office.

52) Ebrahim Z., Irani Z.& Al Shawi S. (2003). e-Government adoption: Analysis of adoption staged models. 3nd European Conference on E-Government.

53) Elmagarmid A. K.& McIver W. J. (2001). The ongoing march toward digital government. IEEE Journal of Computer.

54) Elsas A. (2003). Integration of e-Government and e-Commerce with Web Services. . Springer Berlin Heidelberg. In Electronic Government.

55) Fabisiak L. (2012). Metoda oceny użyteczności serwisów internetowych. praca doktorska . Szczecin, Szczecin, Poland.

56) Fabisiak L. (2013). Ocena uzytecznosci serwisów internetowych na podstawie dzienników logów.Rating usefulness of websites based on logs . , Bydgoszcz

2013,. Polskie Stowarzyszenie Zarzadzania Wiedza, Studia i materiały nr 64, Polish Association of Knowledge Management, Studies and Materials No. 64.

57) Fabisiak L.& Wolski W. (2010). Metody analizy wielokryterialnej w ocenie użyteczności serwisów internetowych,. Zarządzanie wiedzą w warunkach kryzysu finansowego gospodarki, Materiały Polskiego Stowarzyszenia Zarządzania Wiedzą.

58) Falahrastegar M., Haddadi H., Uhlig S.& Mortier R. (2014). The rise of panopticons: Examining region-specific third-party web tracking. In Traffic Monitoring and Analysis (pp. 104-114). Springer Berlin Heidelberg.

59) Fang X.& Liu Sheng O. R. (2005). Designing a better web portal for digital government: a web-mining based approach. Digital Government Society of North America.

60) Filutowicz Z.& Przybyszewski K. (2014). Analysis Of Customer Requirements For Example Of Electronic Systems Index. Analiza Wymagań Uïytkowników Na Przykładzie Systemów Elektronicznego Indeksu.Polish article. Instytut Technologii Informatycznych, pszw.edu.pl.

61) Fjeldstad O. H.& Heggstad K. (2012). Local government revenue mobilisation in Anglophone Africa.

62) Flak L. S., Moe C. E.& Sæbø, Ø. (2003). On the evolution of e-government: The user imperative. In Electronic Government. Springer Berlin Heidelberg.

63) Fogli D. Colosio, S.& Sacco M. (2010). Managing accessibility in local e-government websites through end-user development: a case study. Springer, Universal Access in the Information Society.

64) Foley N. S., Corless R., Escapa M., Fahy F., Fernandez-Macho, J., Gabriel, S.& Tinch, D. (2015). Developing a Comparative Marine Socio-Economic Framework for the European Atlantic Area. Journal of Ocean and Coastal Economics, 2014(1), 3.

65) Fountain J. E. (2004). Building the virtual state: Information technology and institutional change. USA: Brookings Institution Press.

66) Friend J.& Jessop N. (2013). Local Government and Strategic Choice (Routledge Revivals): An Operational Research Approach to the Processes of Public Planning. Routledge.

67) Gamper J. & Augsten N. (2003). The Role of Web Services in Digital Government. Springer EGOV.

68) Gamper J. & Augsten N. (2003). The role of web services in digital government. In Electronic Government. Springer Berlin Heidelberg.

69) Garnik I. (2006). Vendor credibility in e-shops design in Poland: an empirical study. . In Proceedings of the 13th Eurpoean conference on Cognitive ergonomics: trust and control in complex socio-technical systems.

70) Garrett J. J. (2002). The Elements of User Experience: User-Centered Design for the web. New Riders Press, Third Edition.

71) Gębarowski M. (2013). The Evaluation Of Websites Of Polish Cities In The Context Of Their Usability. International conference 2013. Croatia: Management and knowledge learning.

72) Gichoya D. (2005). Factors affecting the successful implementation of ICT projects in government. Electronic Journal of e-government.

73) Gilbert & Richard. (2013). Making Cities Work: Role of Local Authorities in the Urban Environment. Routledge.

74) Goldkuhl G. & Persson A. (2006). From e-ladder to e-diamond-re-conceptualising models for public e-services. ECIS.

75) Gomes R. & Sousa L. (2012). Contributions to the Development of Local e-Government 2.0. Future Internet.

76) González F. & Miranda. (2004). Quantitative evaluation of commercial web sites: an empirical study of Spanish firms. International Journal of Information Management Elsevier.

77) Goodwin S., Burford N., Bedard M., Carrigan E.& Hannigan G. C. (2006.). CMS/CMS: content management system/change management strategies. Library Hi Tech.

78) Gregory D., Streib K. & Willougbby G. (2001). The future of local government administration, local governments Becoming e-government: Getting the Sizzle, Avoiding the Fizzle. USA.

79) Guo X. & Lu J. (2004). Effectiveness of e-government online services in Australia. Digital Government: Strategies and Implementation from Developing and Developed Countries.. Idea Group Inc.

80) Hackos J. (2002). Content Management for Dynamic Web Delivery , 1st edition, Wiley, 2002. In J. Hackos, Content Management for Dynamic Web Delivery (Paperback), 1st edition. New York, NY, USA: John Wiley & Sons, Inc.

81) Hellwig Z. (1968). Zastosowanie metody taksonomicznej do typologicznego podziału krajów ze względu na poziom ich rozwoju oraz zasoby i strukturę wykwalifikowanych kadr. . Przegląd statystyczny.

82) Helmut D. (2005). Local Electronic Government A comparative study. In H. Drüke, Local Electronic Government (p. 283). London And New York: Routledge.

83) Henriksson& Anders. (2007). Evaluation instrument for e-government websites.. Electronic Government, an International Journal 4.2.

84) Ho C. I.& Lee Y. L. (2007). The development of an e-travel service quality scale. , 28(6), 1434–1449. Tourism Management,elsevier.

85) Holzinger A. (2005). Usability Engineering Methods for Software Developers. . Communications of the ACM, Vol. 48, No. 1.

86) Hom J. (1998). The usability methods toolbox handbook.

87) Hong H. (2013). Government websites and social media's influence on government-public relationships. Public Relations Review.

88) Hoogwout & Marcel. (2003). Super pilots, subsidizing or self-organization: stimulating e-government initiatives in Dutch local governments.". Springer Berlin Heidelberg, Electronic Government.

89) Horan T. A., Abhichandani T. & Rayalu R. (2006). Assessing user satisfaction of e-government services: development and testing of quality-in-use satisfaction with advanced traveler information systems (ATIS). In System Sciences, HICSS'0 Proceedings of the 39th Annual Hawaii International Conference . , Vol. 4.

90) Huang W. (2005). Electronic Government Strategies and Implementations. USA: Idea Group Inc.

91) Huizingh E. K. (2000). The content and design of web sites: an empirical study.. Information and Management , 37(3).

92) Institute for local government (2012). Local Agency Website Transparency Opportunities. USA.

93) IsaW. A., Noor N. L. & Mehad S. (2009). Cultural Prescription vs. User Perception of Information Architecture for Culture Centered Website: A Case Study on Muslim Online User. Springer, Proceeding of HCII2009.

94) Jamak   A., Saridan   A. & Zulkipli R. (2011). Transformation Building of Microentrepreneurs: A Conceptual Model. World Academy of Science, Engineering and Technology International Journal of Social, Education, Economics and Management Engineering.

95) James K. (2008). Projektowanie nawigacji strony WWW: optymalizacja funkcjonalnoci witryny. Poland: Helion.

96) Jaspers M. W. (2009). A comparison of usability methods for testing interactive health technologies: Methodological aspects and empirical evidence. international journal of medical informatics 78, Elsevier Ireland Ltd, Academic Medical Center- University of Amsterdam, Amsterdam, The Netherlands.

97) JATI H. (2010). Hybrid Approach for Website Quality Evaluation: Linear Weightage Model and Fuzzy Analytical Hierarchy Process. Doctoral dissertation . Universiti Teknologi PETRONAS.

98) Jeffries R. & Heather D. (1992). Usability testing vs. heuristic evaluation: was there a contest? ACM SIGCHI Bulletin.

99) Johnson-Eilola. (2002). Designing effective Web sites: A concise guide. Boston: Houghton Mifflin.

100) Johnston M. (2013, 03 07). CMS or WCM - Which is Which? Retrieved 09 07, 2014, from www.cmscritic.com.: http://www.cmscritic.com/cms-or-wcm-which-is-which/

101) Journal Public Procurement Law. (2004). General Provisions. Poland.

102) Kaaya J. (2001). Implementing e-government services in East Africa: Assessing status through content analysis of . Electronic Journal of e-Government Volume 2 Issue 1.

103) Kallas Z. (2011). Butchers' preferences for rabbit meat; AHP Pairwise comparisons versus a LIKERT scale valuation. . In Proceedings of the 11st International Symposium on the Analytic Hierarchy Process and Analytic Network Process [ISAHP 2011].

104) Kantner L.& Rosenbaum S. (1997). Usability Studies of WWW Sites: Heuristic Evaluation vs. Laboratory Testing. International Conference on Computer Documentation (pp. pp 153-160). New York,USA: ACM SIGDOC'97,Snowbird.

105) Karkin N. & Janssen M. (2014). Evaluating websites from a public value perspective: A review of Turkish local government websites. . International Journal of Information Management.

106) Karwatka T. (2009). Usability w e-biznesie: co kieruje twoim klientem? Helion.

107) Kasperski M. & Boguska-Torbicz A. (2008). Projektowanie stron WWW, ISBN. Użyteczność w praktyce, Helion.

108) Kathuria G. (2006). Web content management with documentum. Birmingham, UK.: Packt Publishing Ltd.

109) Kaushik A. (2009). Godzina dziennie z Web Analytics. Stwórz dobrą strategię e-marketingowa. Poland, Gliwice, P7: Helion, , In Polish.

110) Ke W.& Wei K. K. (2004). Successful e-government in Singapore. Communications of the ACM.

111) Kelton A. S.& Yang Y. W. (2008). The impact of corporate governance on Internet financial reporting. Journal of accounting and Public Policy.

112) Kelton S.& Pennington R. (2012). Internet financial reporting: The effects of information presentation format and content differences on investor decision making. Computers in Human Behavior.

113) Kim, H. J. & Bretschneider S. (2004). Local government information technology capacity: an exploratory theory. IEEE, Proceedings of the 37th Annual Hawaii International Conference.

114) Kim H. N., Kavanaugh A.& Smith-Jackson T. L. (2007). Implementation of Internet technology for local government website: Design guidelines. In System Sciences, 2007. HICSS 2007. 40th Annual Hawaii International Conference on (pp. 93-93). IEEE.

115) Kim S. & Lee J. (2012). E-Participation, Transparency, and Trust in Local Government. Wiley Online Library, Public Administration Review.

116) King A. (2008). Website optimization. "O'Reilly Media, Inc.".

117) Kleijnen S.& Raju, S. (2003). An open web services architecture. Queue.

118) Kolenda M. (2006). Taksonomia numeryczna. Prace Naukowe Akademii Ekonomicznej we Wrocławiu. Seria: . Monografie i Opracowania.

119) Kolsaker A. & Lee-Kelley L. (2008). Citizens' attitudes towards e-government and e-governance: a UK study. International Journal of Public Sector Management.

120) Kopackova H., Michalek K. & Cejna K. (2010). Accessibility and findability of local e-government websites in the Czech Republic. Universal access in the information society.

121) Kowalczyk A. (2000). Local government in Poland. Decentralization: experiments and reforms.

122) Krishnan   S. & Teo T. S. (2012). Moderating effects of governance on information infrastructure and e-government development. Journal of the American Society for Information Science and Technology.

123) Kukuła K. (2000). Metoda unitaryzacji zerowanej. . Wydaw. Naukowe PWN.

124) Kwak   Y. H., Chih   Y. & Ibbs, C. W. (2009). Towards a comprehensive understanding of public private partnerships for infrastructure development. California Management Review.

125) Laswad F., Fisher R. & Oyelere P. (2005). Determinants of voluntary Internet financial reporting by local government authorities. . Journal of Accounting and Public Policy.

126) Law R., Shanshan Q. & and Dimitrios B. "Progress in tourism management: A review of website evaluation in tourism research." Tourism management 31.3 (2010): 297-313.

127) Lazar J., Dudley-Sponaugle A.& Kisha-Dawn G. "Improving web accessibility: a study of webmaster perceptions." Computers in Human Behavior 20.2 (2004): 269-288.

128) Léautier F. A. (2006). Cities in a Globalizing World. Governance, Performance & Sustainability. WBI Learning Research Series. Washington DC.: The World Bank Institute. The Word Bank.

129) Lee Y. & Kenneth A. K. (2006). Investigating the effect of website quality on e-business success: An analytic hierarchy process (AHP) approach Decision Support Systems. Elsevier. , PP1383–1401, P4, United state.

130) Lee Y.& Kozar K. A. (2012). Understanding of website usability: Specifying and measuring constructs and their relationships. Elsevier, Decision Support Systems.

131) Lowe C. (2003). Experiences of Take-up of E-Government in Europe. Springer.

132) Makki K. S. & Leppert G. (2006). Factors of usability design for multilingual and multicultural websites. In Information Reuse and Integration. IEEE International Conference.

133) Margetts H. & Dunleavy P. (2002). Better Public Services through e-government Academic Article in support of Better Public Services through e-government. National Audit Office.

134) Maristella M., Francesca R.& Giovanni T. C. (2013). Web Usability: Principles and Evaluation Methods. springer, Department of Electronics and Information,Politecnico di Milano.

135) McDermott I. (2008). Joomla! Looms: Can open source CMS save a library website. Searcher.

136) McKeever S. (2003). Understanding web content management systems: evolution, lifecycle and market. . Industrial Management & Data Systems.

137) Meurs M. & Kochut R. (2013). Local Government Performance in Rural Poland: The Roles of Local Government Characteristics and Inherited Conditions. American University, Washington, DC.

138) Mican D., Tomai N., & Coroş R. I. (2009). Web Content Management Systems, a Collaborative Environment in the Information Society. Faculty of Economics and Business Administration, Babeş-Bolyai University, Informatica Economică vol.13, Romania.

139) Mimicopoulos M. G., Kyj L., Sormani, N., Bertucci, G., & Qian, H. (2007). Public Governance Indicators: A Literature Review. New York: Department of Economic and Social Affairs.

140) Minocha S., Dawson L., Roberts D., & Petre M. (2004/12). E-SEQUAL: A Customer-Centred Approach to Providing Value in E-Commerce Environments. Technical Report , Department of Computing, The Open University.

141) Moon M. J. (2002). The evolution of e-government among municipalities: rhetoric or reality?. Public administration review. Improving a human-computer dialogue.Communications of the ACM, 33(3), 338-348

142) Morgan J. Q. (2009). The Role of Local Government in Economic Development: Survey Findings from North Carolina . UNC, University of North Carolina School of governance.

143) Morrison A. M., Taylor J. S. & Douglas A. (2005). Website evaluation in tourism and hospitality: the art is not yet stated. . Journal of Travel & Tourism Marketing.

144) Morville P. (1998). Information Architecture on the World Wide Web. USA: O'Reilly & Associates, Inc. First Edition.

145) Morville, P. (2006). Information Architecture on the World Wide Web. USA: O'Reilly & Associates, Inc., Third Edition, February.

146) Morville P. (1998). Information Architecture on the World Wide Web",First edition, P18. USA: O'Reilly & Associates, Inc.

147) Nacar R., & Burnaz S. (2011). A cultural content analysis of multinational companies' web sites. Qualitative Market Research: An International Journal. Emerald.

148) Ndou V. (2004.). E-government for developing countries: opportunities and challenges. The electronic journal of information systems in developing countries.

149) Nermend K. (2009). Taxonomic Synthetic Vector Measure in the Assessment of Regional Development: Results of Empirical Research. Springer.

150) Nermend K. (2009). Vector Calculus in Regional Development Analysis: Comparative Regional Analysis Using the Example of Poland. Poland: Springer Science & Business Media.

151) Nermend K., Wasikowska, B. & Shihab, A. (2013). The application of web-tracking method for research of local government units' websites utility. EEE13, Worldcomp13.

152) Nermend K. (2006). A synthetic measure of sea environment pollution. Polish Journal of Environmetal Studies, Vol. 15 no 4b.

153) Netergistry (2014). The beginner's guide to content management systems. Online under link, http://www.netregistry.com.au/files/getfile.php?f=beginners-guide-online-business.pdf, e-book ,(data:09-06-2015).

154) Nielsen J. (2003). Usability for $200. . Online im Internet. Online verfügbar unter http://www. useit. com/alertbox/20030602. html, zuletzt geprüft am, 16, 2006.

155) Nielsen J. a. (1990). Heuristic evaluation of user interfaces. Proc. ACM CHI'90 Conf.

156) Nielsen J. (2000). Designing web usability: The practice of simplicity. USA: New Riders Publishing.

157) Nielsen J. (1994). HCI: Using discount usability engineering to penetrate the intimidation barrier. Cost-justifying usability. neerci.ist.utl.pt.

158) Nielsen J. (1993). Usability Engineering. Academic Press,Cambridge .

159) Nielsen J. (1994). Usability engineering. Elsevier.

160) Nielsen J.& Loranger, H. (2006). Prioritizing web usability. . Pearson Education.

161) Nielsen J. & Mack R. L. (1994). Usability Inspection Methods. John Wiley & Sons, Inc.

162) Nielsen J. & Pernice K. (2010). Eyetracking Web Usability. . Nielsen Norman Group, Berkeley.

163) Nowakowski M. (2014). Application Of Usability Test For The Analysis Of A Search System In Online Stores. Studia i Materialy Polskiego Stowarzyszenia Zarzadzania Wiedza/Studies & Proceedings Polish Association for Knowledge Management.

164) Owsiski J.& Ponichtera, R. (2010). Local Web-Based Networks Centred On Self-Governmental Websites Vs. Local Activity–A Project Outline1. Polish Association For Knowledge Management, Series: Studies & Proceedings No. 34.

165) Parasuraman A. , Zeithaml V. & Berry L. (1988). SERVQUAL: A Multiple-item Scale for Measuring Consumer Perceptions of Service Quality. Journal of Retailing, Vol. 64, No. 1.

166) Parasuraman A., Zeithaml V.& Malhotra A. (2005.). E-S-QUAL A Multiple-Item Scale for Assessing Electronic Service Quality. Journal of Service Research, Vol. 7, No. 10.

167) Parlak B., Sobaci M. Z.& Ökmen M. (2008). The evaluation of restructured local governments in turkey within the context of the european charter on local self-government. Ankara Law Review.

168) Pawel A. & Banas. (2010). International Ideal and Local Practice Access to Environmental Information and Local Government in Poland. Central European University, Budapest, Hungary, Environmental Policy and Governance. , Pol. Gov. 20.

169) Pawlowska A., Litewski P.& Sakowicz M. (2002). ICT in Polish local government – better services, more transparency, prospects for increased participation. Applying the E-government Framework in Transitional Countries, Department of Public administration,Warsaw.

170) Pawlowska A., Litewski P., & Sakowicz M. (2003). ICT in Polish local government–better services, more transparency, prospects for increased participation. Warsaw, Poland: Paper for the Working Group.

171) Morville P. & Rosenfeld L. (2006). Information Architecture on the World Wide Web. USA: O'Reilly & Associates, Inc. p 266.

172) Picot A., & Wernick C. (2007). The role of government in broadband access.Telecommunications Policy, 31(10), 660-674.

173) Plessers P., Casteleyn S., Yesilada Y., De Troyer O., Stevens R., Harper S., (2005.). Accessibility: a web engineering approach. In Proceedings of the 14th international conference on World Wide Web.

174) Poltrock S. & Grudin J. (1994). Organizational obstacles to interface and development. ACM , Transactions on Computer Human Interaction.

175) Prabhu C. S. (2013). E-governance: Concepts and case studies. . PHI Learning Pvt. Ltd.

176) Prasad, A., & Shivarajan, S. (2015). Understanding the role of technology in reducing corruption: a transaction cost approach. Wiley Online Library, Journal of Public Affairs.

177) Rafal S., & David T. (2011). Public-private Partnerships in Poland:Public - Privat E Partnershipssuccesses And Failures. Overcoming Psychological Barriers and Rigid Regulation, Budapest, Hungary.

178) Rahim W. W., Rashideen S. M., & Ilyani, S. N. (2010). Evaluating the Accessibility of Malaysia E-Government Website. In Proceedings of Knowledge Management International Conference (KMICe), Malaysia.

179) Rahman H. (2010). Framework of E-governance at the Local Government Level. In Comparative e-government. Springer New York.

180) Rand P. (2012). PhD Thesis in Towards Designing Localized Websites . The Cultural Conceptual Model (C2M) & the LWDA tool: Putting the Cultural Markers Pyramid into Practice. Brussels, Brussels, Belgium: Vrije University Brussel, Faculty of Science and Bio-Engineering Sciences,Department of Computer Science , Research Group: Web & Information System Engineering.

181) Reddick C. G. (2004). A two-stage model of e-government growth: Theories and empirical evidence for US cities. . Elsevier, Government Information Quarterly.

182) Regulski J. (2003). Local Government Reform in Poland: an insider's story., Local Government and Public Service Reform Initiative. Open Society Institute– Budapest .

183) Reinecke K., & Bernstein A. (2013). Knowing what a user likes: A design science approach to interfaces that automatically adapt to culture. . Mis Quarterly.

184) Rek D., & Sulikowski P. (2011). Optymalizacja Interfejsów Sklepów Internetowych A Maksymalizacja Sprzedaży. ebscohost, Studia i Materialy Polskiego Stowarzyszenia Zarzadzania Wiedza/Studies & Proceedings Polish Association for Knowledge Management.

185) Richard V., Steve G., & Stuart B. (2001). Web Content Management. 14th Bled Electronic Commerce Conference, Bled, Slovenia.

186) Rogerson C. M. (2011). Tracking local economic development policy and practice in South Africa, 1994–2009. In Urban Forum (Vol. 22, No. 2, pp. 149-168). Springer Netherlands.

187) Rosenfeld L., & Morville P. (2002). Information architecture for the world wide web. " O'Reilly Media, Inc.".

188) Rosson M. B.& Carroll J. M. (2001). Usability Engineering. Scenario-Based Development of Human-Computer Interaction. USA: Academic press.

189) Rubin J. & Dana C. (2004). How to Plan, Design, and Conduct Effective Tests. John Wiley and Sons, Inc.P39.

190) Russell O'Hare EdD C. R. M. & CBA C. (2015). Taming the Information Explosion with Enterprise Content Management. Information Management,49(3), 36.

191) Sammons M. C. (2004). The internet writer's handbook. New York: Pearson Education.

192) Schelin S. (2007). Local Government Information Technology. Chapel Hill School of Government, County and Municipal Government in North Carolina, USA.

193) Sebek. (2003). Delivering e-government services to citizens and businesses: the government gateway concept. In Electronic Government. Springer Berlin Heidelberg.

194) Seock Y. K. & Chen-Yu J. H. (2007). Website evaluation criteria among US college student consumers with different shopping orientations and Internet channel usage. . Wiley Online Library, International Journal of Consumer Studies.

195) Shariff M. (2010). Alfresco 3 Enterprise Content Management Implementation. USA: Packt Publishing Ltd.

196) Sharlin M., Tu, E.& Bartus T. (2009). Guide to Creating Website Information Architecture and Content. Princeton University.P8.

197) Shatkin. (2000). Obstacles to empowerment: Local politics and civil society in metropolitan Manila,. Urban Studies, the Philippines.

198) Shneiderman B. (1997). Designing information-abundant web sites: issues and recommendations. International Journal of Human-Computer Studies.

199) Sikorski M. (2002). Zastosowanie metody QFD do doskonalenia jakości użytkowej serwisów WWW. Zeszyty Naukowe Politechniki Poznańskiej. Organizacja i Zarządzanie.

200) Sikorski M. (2012). A Cross-Disciplinary UX Evaluation of a CRM System. International Workshop on the Interplay between User Experience and Software Development I-UxSED 2012, Copenhagen, Denmark.

201) Sikorski M. (2009). From user satisfaction to customer loyalty: addressing economic values in user-centered design of on-line services. In Proceedings of the COST-298 Conference 'The Good, the Bad and the Challenging: The User and the Future of Information and Communication Technologies.

202) Sikorski M. (2010). Interakcja człowiek-komputer. Wyd. PJWSTK, Warszawa.

203) Sivaji A., Azween, A., Alan, G.& Downe. (2011). Usability testing methodology: Effectiveness of heuristic evaluation in E-government website development. IEEE.

204) Skica T., Bem A.& Żygadło K. (2013). The Role Of Local Government In The Process Of Entrepreneurship Development. e-Finanse,University of Information Technology and Management, Financial Internet Quarterly , vol. 9/nr 4.

205) Skulimowski A. M. (2008). The Information Society in Poland: recent developments and future perspectives.

206) Smith A. G. (2001). Applying evaluation criteria to New Zealand government websites. International journal of information management, 21(2), 137-149.

207) Smith A. (2010). Government ICT Strategy Smarter, cheaper, greener. Norwich: Crown Book.

208) Staebner A. & Marchand J. P. (2012). Public-private partnership for motorway in Poland: Research at the national and European levels. Research at the national and European levels. ,European Roads Review.

209) Štaud O. (2013). Comparison Of Subsides Of The Sport And Culture Institutions By The Local Government. Academy of Management Journal.

210) Stieger S. & Reips U. D. (2010). What are participants doing while filling in an online questionnaire: A paradata collection tool and an empirical study. Elsevier, Computers in Human Behavior.

211) Streib G. D. & G.Willougbby K. (2002). Future of local government administration, local governments Becoming e- government: Getting the Sizzle, Avoiding the Fizzle ", USA: Georgia state University.

212) Streib G. D. & Katherine G. W. (2005.). Local governments as e-governments: Meeting the implementation challenge. Public Administration Quarterly.

213) Streichsbier C., Blazek P., Faltin F. & Fruhwirt W. (2009). Are De-Facto Standards a Useful Guide for Designing Human-Computer Interaction Processes? The Case of User Interface Design for Web Based B2C Product Configurators. In System Sciences,IEEE.

214) Summers K. & Michael S. (2005). Creating websites that work.Houghton Mifflin.

215) Svensson L. (2012). Design and performance of Small scale sensory consumer tests. stud.epsilon.slu.se.

216) Szeremeta J. (2002). Benchmarking e-government: a global perspective. in. international congress on government on line.

217) Szewczyk A. (2014). Usability Of Internet Shops Quoting The Example Of E-Pharmacies. Studies & Proceedings Polish Association for Knowledge Management.

218) Tan W. S., Liu D.& Bishu R. (2009). Web evaluation: Heuristic evaluation vs. user testing. . International Journal of Industrial Ergonomics.

219) Tarafdar M. & Zhang J. (2008). Determinants of reach and loyalty-a study of Website performance and implications for Website design. Journal of Computer Information Systems.

220) Teoh K. K., OngT. S., Lim P. W., Liong R. P. & Yap C. Y. (2009). Explorations on web usability, American Journal of Applied Sciences.

221) Thompson K. M., Charles R., McClure P., T. &Jaeger T. P.(2003). Evaluating federal websites: Improving e-government for the people. Computers in society: Privacy, ethics, and the Internet.

222) Tsai W. H., Chou W. C.& Lai C. W. (2010). An effective evaluation model and improvement analysis for national park websites: A case study of Taiwan. . Tourism Management.

223) Unit. U. e.-G. (2003). Quality Framework for UK Government Website Design: Usability issues for government websites. UK: Guidelines for UK government websites.

224) UNDPEPA (2002). Benchmarking e-Government: A Global Perspective, Assessing the Progress of the UN Member States.

225) Ustawa. (1998). Law , Act of 5, No. 91, item.578, as amended. Poland: county government.

226) Ustawa PZP. (2004). Ustawa z dnia 29 stycznia 2004 r. Prawo zamówień publicznych, amended Dz. U. z 2010 r. Nr 113, poz. 759 z późn. zm, In engilish ... The Act of 29 January 2004. Public Procurement Law Journal. Laws of 2010. item. 759.

227) Verlinden J. C. & Coenders M. J. (2000). Qualitative usability measurement of websites by employing the repertory grid technique. ACM, In CHI'00 Extended Abstracts on Human Factors in Computing Systems.

228) Wagner C., Cheung K. S., Ip R. K. & Bottcher S. (2005). Building Semantic Webs for e-government with Wiki technology. Electronic Government, an International Journal, 3(1), 36-55.

229) Wagner S. (2003). London, Routledge. Understanding Green Consumer Behaviour: A Qualitative, Cognitive Approach.

230) Wang L., Bretschneider S. & Gant J. (2005). Evaluating web-based e-government services with a citizen-centric approach. Wang, L., Bretschneider, S., & Gant, J. (2005, January). Evaluating web-based e-government services with a citizen-

centric approach. In System IEEE, Sciences, 2005. HICSS'05. Proceedings of the 38th Annual Hawaii International Conference.

231) Wang Q. (2011). Usability research of interaction design for e-commerce Website. IEEE, In E-Business and E-Government (ICEE).

232) Warf B. (2013.). Global E-Government. Global Geographies of the Internet. Springer Netherlands.

233) Weerakkod (2009). Social and Organizational Developments through Emerging E-Government Applications: New Principles and Concepts: New Principles and Concepts. Hershey , New York: IGI Global.

234) Williams M. & Beynon-Davies P. (2004). Implementing e-Government in the UK: An analysis of local-level strategies. AMCIS.

235) Wilson D. & Game C. (2011). Local government in the United Kingdom. . Palgrave Macmillan.

236) Yavuz N. & Welch E. W. (2014). Factors affecting openness of local government websites: Examining the differences across planning, finance and police departments. Government Information Quarterly, 31(4), 574-583.

237) Yoo B. & Donthu N. (2001). Developing a Scale to Measure the Perceived Quality of An Internet Shopping Site (SITEQUAL). Quartely Journal of Electronic Commerce, No. 2.

238) Younghwa L., Kenneth A. & Kozar. (2006). Investigating the effect of website quality on e-business success: An analytic hierarchy process (AHP) approach. Decision Support Systems, Elsevier.

239) Zambrano R. (2010). E-Governance and Development: Service Delivery to Empower the Poor. USA: United Nations Development Program, , Book in IGI Global.

240) Zambrano R. (2009). E-governance and development: Service delivery to empower the poor. Social and Organizational Developments through Emerging E-Government Applications: . New Principles and Concepts.

241) Zeithaml V., Parasuraman A.& Malhotra A. (2002). Service Quality Delivery Through Web Sites: A Critical Review of Extant Knowledge. Journal of the Academy of Marketing Science, Vol. 30, No. 4.

242) Zhang P.& Von D. G. (2001). Expectations and rankings of Web site quality features: Results of two studies on user perceptions. IEEE, In System Sciences, 2001.Proceedings of the 34th Hawaii International Conference on System Sciences.

243) Zhang P. & von D. G. (2002). User Expectations and Rankings of Quality Factors in Different Web Site Domains. Internetional Journal of Electronic Commerce, Vol. 6, No.2.

244) ZhengF. & Lu Y. (2012). Influencing Factors of Public Satisfaction in Local Governments' Overall Performance Evaluation in China. IEEE, Business Intelligence and Financial Engineering (BIFE), 2012 Fifth International Conference.

245) Zhenxiang S. & Huaihe C. (2010). An accessibility study of Chinese local government websites. IEEE, International Conference on Networking and Digital Society.

246) Zhou Q. & DeSantis R. (2005). Usability issues in city tourism Web site design: a content analysis. . In Professional Communication Conference IEEE, IPCC.

247) Zhou Y. X. (2009). Usage-Centered Design for Government Websites-A Practical Analysis to Canada Government Website. IEEE , Vol. 1.

248) Ziemba E. (2005). Metodologia budowy serwisów internetowych dla zastosowań gospodarczych. Prace Naukowe/Akademia Ekonomiczna w Katowicach.

249) Ziemba E. (2009). Projektowanie portali korporacyjnych dla organizacji opartych na wiedzy, Katowicach: Wydawnictwo Uniwersytetu Ekonomicznego w Katowicach.

250) Ziemba E. (2005). The methodology of building websites for business use. Katowice: Work Research / University of Economics in Katowice.

251) Ziemba E., Papaj T.& Descours D. (2014a). Assessing the quality of e-government portals-the Polish experience. In Computer Science and Information Systems (FedCSIS), 2014 Federated Conference . IEEE.

252) Ziemba E., Papaj T.& Descours D. (2014). Factors Affecting Success of e-Government Portals: A Perspective of Software Quality Model. In Proceedings of European Conference on eGovernment.

253) Ziemba E., Papaj T.& Descours D. (2014b). Factors Affecting Success of e-Government Portals: A Perspective of Software Quality Model. European Conference on eGovernment. Brasov, Romania: Spiru Haret University.

254) Ziemba P. (2013). Integracja metod oceny jakości serwisów internetowych z wykorzystaniem ontologii,. praca doktorska . Szczecin, Poland.

255) Ziemba P., & Budzińsk i. R. (2011). Dobór kryteriów dla oceny serwisów informacyjnych w portalach internetowych,. Studia i Materiały Polskiego Stowarzyszenia Zarządzania Wiedzą, Nr 37.

256) Ziemba P. & Budziński R. (2010). Ontologies in integration of websites evaluation methods. Information Systems in Management VI. WULS Press, Warszawa.

257) Ziemba P. & Piwowarski M. (2010). Metody oceny jakości portali internetowych. . Studia i Materiały Polskiego Stowarzyszenia Zarządzania Wiedzą 27.

258) Ziemba P., Piwowarski M., Jankowski J. & Wątróbski J. (2014). Method of Criteria Selection and Weights Calculation in the Process of Web Projects Evaluation. Computational Collective Intelligence. Technologies and Applications. Springer International Publishing.

www.ingramcontent.com/pod-product-compliance
Lightning Source LLC
Chambersburg PA
CBHW041151050326
40690CB00001B/432

* 9 7 8 1 9 8 6 4 9 4 8 0 9 *